SAM ALLBERRY
JAMES FOR YOU

thegoodbook
COMPANY

James For You

© Sam Allberry, 2015.
Reprinted 2017, 2018, 2019, 2020.

thegoodbook
COMPANY

Published by:
The Good Book Company

thegoodbook.com | www.thegoodbook.co.uk
thegoodbook.com.au | thegoodbook.co.nz | thegoodbook.co.in

ISBN: 9781910307793

Printed in India

Design by André Parker

CONTENTS

SERIES PREFACE

Each volume of the *God's Word For You* series takes you to the heart of a book of the Bible, and applies its truths to your heart.

The central aim of each title is to be:

- Bible centred
- Christ glorifying
- Relevantly applied
- Easily readable

You can use *James For You:*

To read. You can simply read from cover to cover, as a book that explains and explores the themes, encouragements and challenges of this part of Scripture.

To feed. You can work through this book as part of your own personal regular devotions, or use it alongside a sermon or Bible-study series at your church. Each chapter is divided into two shorter sections, with questions for reflection at the end of each.

To lead. You can use this as a resource to help you teach God's word to others, both in small-group and whole-church settings. You'll find tricky verses or concepts explained using ordinary language, and helpful themes and illustrations along with suggested applications.

These books are not commentaries. They assume no understanding of the original Bible languages, nor a high level of biblical knowledge. Verse references are marked in **bold** so that you can refer to them easily. Any words that are used rarely or differently in everyday language outside the church are marked in grey when they first appear, and are explained in a glossary towards the back. There, you'll also find details of resources you can use alongside this one, in both personal and church life.

Our prayer is that as you read, you'll be struck not by the contents of this book, but by the book it's helping you open up; and that you'll praise not the author of this book, but the One he is pointing you to.

Carl Laferton, Series Editor

INTRODUCTION TO JAMES

The letter of James has strong claims to be both the most celebrated and most criticised of all New Testament books. This alone makes it worthy of close attention—we are unlikely to be left unaffected by it! It has generated enormous controversy among Christians over the years. Some early believers questioned its inclusion in the New Testament. Centuries later, the great Reformer Martin Luther famously described James as "an epistle of straw".

A quick glance at the letter shows us why some have found it to be so problematic. Generally, if you flick through any other New Testament letter, you will likely see the words "Christ" and "Jesus" appearing multiple times on every page. But James seems to have precious little to say about Jesus. Jesus is explicitly mentioned only twice. Given that one of those times comes as James introduces himself at the start of the letter, that leaves only one mention in the entire body of the whole epistle. It's therefore not surprising to find little is also said of Jesus' death and resurrection, two central and defining events for Christian belief and living. So we might worry that this is not going to be a particularly gospel-centred letter. (This suspicion is not helped when we discover the Dalai Lama is particularly drawn to this letter because of what he believes to be its deep resonance with the teaching of Buddhism!)

Others have criticised James for a lack of cohesion. The letter (so they say) seems to chop and change subject from paragraph to paragraph, with no obvious overarching structure or agenda. Paul at least is linear in his writing. The book of James has been dismissed as random snippets of instruction with no apparent rationale.

But perhaps the most famous criticism levelled at James is that he contradicts Paul. It even looks as though James is setting out to do this intentionally, taking one of Paul's cherished teachings—that we are justified by faith alone—and then seemingly turning it on its head by writing: "You see that a person is considered righteous by what they do *and not by faith alone*" (2:24, my emphasis). This was enough for Luther to fume that: "James mangles the Scriptures and thereby opposes Paul and all Scripture". Strong words! Needless to say, those looking for evidence that the Bible is not the inspired word of God leap on this verse with delight.

But we should not be too fast to dismiss this book. Despite the criticisms made against it, this letter has persistently found its way into the hearts and affections of countless Christians through the ages, and it remains one of the most cherished books of the Bible. When we read it carefully and expectantly, it is not hard to see why.

> This letter has persistently found its way into the affections of Christians through the ages.

James has a very punchy and direct style. He shoots from the hip. He tends not to get bogged down in lengthy, technical theological exposition. It is not (generally) a letter that leaves you scratching your head or having to look up long words. It is very practical. James addresses everyday issues of living—how we speak, how we should think about wealth or lack of wealth, how to approach conflict, sickness and suffering. It is wonderfully down to earth.

Related to this is the vivid way in which James writes. His text is full of pictures and illustrations, far more than any other letter. It is hard not to get swept along as James describes blazing forests, mighty ships, resilient farmers and wild flowers. These all add to the immediacy of what James writes. They also provide one of the clues as to what makes this letter so valuable.

James' frequent use of everyday illustrations reminds us of someone else, and this is the clue to the letter's enduring value to Christians in every age.

James was the half-brother of Jesus. And herein lies a tale. The biological connection provided James with no natural advantage or inside track. One of the first things we hear of Jesus' brothers is that they did not believe in him (see John 7:5). Yet by the start of the book of Acts they are listed (with Mary) with those who worshipped alongside Jesus' first disciples. What accounts for this dramatic change? Paul provides the explanation. Following his resurrection, Jesus himself appeared to James (1 Corinthians 15:7). It was not long after this that James became one of the leading Christians in the early church in Jerusalem (see, for example, Acts 21:17-18).

So as we begin to study this letter, we soon realise why its popularity has been so enduring. It is soaked in the words and wisdom of James' older brother. He may not be named much in this letter, but his presence is felt throughout. As we will see, James is every bit as passionate as Paul about Christians living in the light of being justified by faith alone. Yes, James is wide-ranging, and some of the connections between the various parts of his letter are not as obvious as in other New Testament letters. But part of the richness of the Scriptures is that the Holy Spirit did not override the character and style of the writer of each book, but took up those characters and styles and used them to breathe out God's word.

So, whether we are attracted or troubled by all its apparent quirks, James' letter demands our attention for one monumental reason. It is all about what it means truly to follow the "glorious Lord Jesus Christ" (2:1). It will show us what genuine faith looks like in real life—and it will challenge us about how real faith works hard and lives distinctively. James' aim is that his readers would serve Jesus more wholeheartedly and radically, and that must be our goal; and it is my prayer as you read this book that you will find yourself both excited about and enabled to follow more closely James' brother and our Lord.

1. JOY IN TRIALS

James gives every impression of being a writer in a hurry. He doesn't linger at the start of his letter, warming his readers up gently before getting down to business. Instead, he gives the briefest of greetings and gets straight into things. Top of his agenda are trials and how we respond to them, and right away we see what kind of letter this is: practical, pithy and very direct. But before James gets stuck into the issue of trials, we need to take a look at how he introduces himself and his readers.

Introductions

It was the custom in ancient letters to begin by introducing yourself, and James does this by describing himself as: "a servant of God and of the Lord Jesus Christ" (**1:1***). This is what really matters. He has come to know God through the work of Jesus, and finds himself now living wholly for them both. Though James is the younger brother of Jesus, far more important than that biological connection is the spiritual one he enjoys. More significant than being the younger brother of Jesus is being one of his people. And the sign of being one of his people is that we devote ourselves to his service.

The identity of James' readership—"the twelve tribes scattered among the nations" (**v 1**)—looks a little less obvious. The "twelve tribes" is how the people of God were described in the Old Testament. That James further describes them as the "scattered" twelve tribes helps us pinpoint whom he has in mind. The Jews of this time who

---

* All James verse references being looked at in each chapter are in **bold**.

lived outside of Israel thought of themselves in such terms, scattered as they were throughout the Roman world. This strongly suggests that James is writing to Jewish Christians outside of Israel, and fits in with his role as the leader of the predominantly Jewish church in Jerusalem.

But though Jewish Christians of the first century were the primary audience James was writing to, the letter is not restricted to them. It has been preserved in Scripture to bless and nourish Christian believers in all times and places. As we understand what James' words would have meant for them, we can quickly **discern*** what they mean for us. In this secondary sense, then, we find the letter is very much for us as well.

Following the briefest of greetings, James gets straight into his agenda: **trials**. "Consider it pure joy, my brothers and sisters, whenever you face trials of many kinds" (**v 2**).

> James offers us the prospect not just of scraping through trials, but of growing in our trials.

The key here is to see that James says "whenever". Not if, but when. Trials are normal. They are not unexpected or freak occurrences. They are, sadly, part and parcel of the regular Christian life.

But they are not a reality we welcome. Many of us will have experienced times when things seemed as if they couldn't get any worse, only to watch in horror as they did. It may be that for some reading this right now, this is how life seems at the moment. We feel overwhelmed. It doesn't matter if the trials are primarily physical, social, relational, or spiritual; we wonder if we will be able to keep going.

James' plea to us, whatever our situation, is to not let such times finish us as Christians. In fact, just a few verses later, he offers us the prospect not just of scraping through trials, but of actually growing as

---

* Words in grey are defined in the Glossary (page 165).

Christians in our trials: "**Blessed** is the one who **perseveres** under trial because, having stood the test, that person will receive the crown of life that the Lord has promised to those who love him" (v 12). This is a mouth-watering prospect: persevering and receiving wonderful blessing from God at the end of it all. We want to be the person who "perseveres under trial" and who has "stood the test".

But it can feel like only a remote possibility. It sounds like the kind of Christian many of us worry we are not. How can we become someone who perseveres, stands firm in **faith** through hard times, and knows blessing from God in our suffering present and eternal future? That is exactly what James shows us in these opening verses.

Consider it Pure Joy

The first thing we need to do is "consider it pure joy" (**v 2**).

Notice James says: "Consider". He is not telling us so much how to feel as how to think. He is not saying: *Pretend this is fun.* Nor is he calling us always to have a sickly grin or stiff upper lip. As scholars Craig Blomberg and Mariam Kamell put it:

> "James does not command us to wear our 'happy faces' that so many seem to think are required in church or in other Christian circles." (*James,* page 59)

No, James is telling us to think about our trials in a certain way. There is a point of view we need to adopt, a particular way to consider what is going on.

Notice too that James talks of trials of "many kinds". There is a whole range of trials that James has in mind. As we read through the letter, we get a feel for some of the trials James' readers were facing at this point in time—poverty, injustice, conflict, sickness and grief. But James deliberately keeps his language general, and it is great that he does. It is easy when undergoing hardship to think that our particular situation is different to everybody else's, that the normal rules don't apply, and that we are the exception to the rest. But by keeping his language broad, James is showing us that what he is about to say applies to us all. If he had specified a particular trial he had in mind, it would be too easy for the rest of us facing different situations to excuse ourselves from what he is saying. But James' advice is not just for one or two specific situations; it is for trials of "many kinds". Whatever yours might be, this applies to you. James says there is a way to think about it that can bring joy. We will actually be robbing ourselves of joy if we ignore what he is about to say.

Reaching Maturity and Completion

James explains this thinking in **verses 3-4**.

In one sense, his point is straightforward: trials teach us to persevere (**v 3**). They put us in situations where it is not easy to keep going, and where we will only do so with a measure of determination. And perseverance is the means to a wonderful end: that we be "mature and complete, not lacking anything" (**v 4**). James is talking about being rounded and formed as a Christian, growing into the very people we were created and saved to be.

If we stop and think about it, this is actually what we most long for as Christians (or at least what we should most long for): to become more whole in Christ; to know him more fully and intimately. And it is trials that give us this opportunity to mature in our faith. In fact, we can't get there without trials. They are the spiritual equivalent of **growbags**.

This is how the Christian life works; faith grows through learning to persevere in hardship. The **apostle** Paul says something similar in his letter to the Roman church: "We also glory in our sufferings, because we know that suffering produces perseverance; perseverance, character; and character, hope" (Romans 5:3-4).

It is suffering that proves, strengthens and deepens our faith. Faith is a little like a muscle in the human body. It is as it is worked out that it grows. It needs something to push against. Physical training is a painful and sweaty process. The Hollywood actor preparing to play the superhero does not become ready by lazing around and being inactive. Muscle growth requires discomfort. Faith needs the pushback of trials for us to grow spiritually. Trials and difficulties are an opportunity to cling on to the promises of God more tightly.

This is a humbling lesson for us, for it reminds us that we need maturing as Christians. We all have further to grow up and move on in the Christian life. There is no room for being smug. God is not after just a little bit of change in our lives. And if all we pursue is comfort, we will never become truly mature in our faith.

The Most Valuable Thing on Earth

Yet as well as humbling us, this is also a great encouragement for us. It assures us that there is a purpose for our trials. They are not for nothing, and they are never wasted experiences. Why? Because God is achieving something in us as we persevere through them. He is investing in our faith. The British pastor and friend of D.L. Moody, F.B. Meyer, once said that trials are God's vote of confidence in us. None of this means they are not painful. We are not to pretend trials and grief do not hurt us; it is natural and normal that they do, and it would be a denial of our humanity to think we should be immune to the pains of hardship in our lives and in the lives of others. Pain is our reflex reaction to trials, and it is entirely legitimate. Nor is James saying we should go out looking for hardship: that we should deliberately create situations in which we will suffer. No—suffering in and of itself is not a good thing. James *is* saying that it is what God can accomplish through suffering that is good, not the suffering itself. It is an opportunity to gain the most valuable thing on earth: a faith that is complete and lacking nothing; maturity and depth in our relationship with God.

> Suffering is an opportunity to gain the most valuable thing on earth.

There are any number of trials a Christian might have to face. In any typical church fellowship, there will be some people experiencing bereavement, the agonies of broken relationship or a lack of relationship. There will be instances of family breakdown, of long-term and serious health issues, of depression and of temptation. In some cases, there will be suffering caused by things that have happened in the past, things that have been done to individuals that have left deep and long-term scars, and also things that individuals have done to others that continue to haunt them. That's the reality of life in this world, as it was for James' first readers.

But through all this, James' counsel is to consider it pure joy. As Christians, we are to think about trials in the light of what God is achieving in us through them, in light of the prospect trials afford for us to surge ahead in our relationship with him. We are to cherish the prospect of a deeper and richer faith.

This is wonderful wisdom. One of the features of trials is that they so often become all-consuming. It can be hard to think about anything else. We can become utterly absorbed by what we are going through, and it can seem impossible to look beyond the immediacy of the pain in order to see anything else. It is even possible to become desensitised to the pains of others who are close. Suffering can so easily turn us in on ourselves.

And so the battle is with the will. James is not saying that Christians will automatically be able to experience joy in suffering. We are called to "consider" trials in this way. We need to fight to think about them in the right way: consciously to force our perspective and vision above and beyond the present suffering, so that we look forward to the good that God will, over time, produce through them. It is as we do this that, alongside the deep pain, we can have a sense of the presence and goodness of God, and be assured that we are in his hands and that he is at work within us.

And above all, we can relish the pulse-quickening promise that God is using such trials to make us more and more like Jesus Christ.

Questions for reflection

1. How do you tend to think about trials? How realistic did verse 2 seem to you when you first read it in this chapter?

2. How about now?

3. "The battle is with the will." Is there a way you need to fight to consider a trial a joy? How will you use verses 3-4 in order to do so?

PART TWO

What to do in a Trial

Trials give us the opportunity to grow, but that does not mean we will know what to do. If we are to discern what God is teaching us through trials—how to conduct ourselves and how best to live—we will need wisdom.

During times of intense pain, it is common to feel a sense of disorientation, to lose our bearings. I remember one friend in the midst of suffering saying that it felt as if he didn't know which way was up anymore. He felt a sense of paralysis and didn't know what he was supposed to do. Another friend also in the thick of difficulties once sent an email where he simply admitted: "I just don't know the Lord's way through this". Trials and confusion tend to go together.

We see this connection a number of times in the Bible. In Psalm 25, David wrestles with overwhelming opposition from his enemies and profound guilt due to his own sin. In the midst of these trials, we see him praying fervently for God's guidance: "Show me your ways, Lord, teach me your paths. Guide me in your truth and teach me" (Psalm 25:4-5). Similarly, it is as Paul reflects on our suffering in this life that he writes: "We do not know what we ought to pray for" (Romans 8:26).

So it is no surprise that, having given us our first piece of counsel ("Consider it pure joy", James **1:2**), James now turns to our need for wisdom. "If any of you lacks **wisdom**, you should ask God, who gives generously to all without finding fault, and it will be given to you" (**v 5**).

> We do not need to feel that trials are times we have to prove we have it all figured out.

James knows that at times when we feel that we need it the most, we often lack wisdom. So we are to come to God. It is that simple. We do not need to feel that, in the middle of trials, this is a time when we have to prove ourselves—to show God that we've been paying attention in class and now have it all figured out. It is OK to need guidance.

Trials in the Christian life are not times when we're supposed to know exactly what to do, when all our training is supposed to kick in. James assumes both that we will need wisdom and yet we lack wisdom. That's why he counsels us to ask God for it. We are supposed to feel that we need divine help. It is healthy at these times to realise how much we don't know. We're not letting anyone down. In fact, as is so often the case with prayer, we find that God is far more willing to answer our prayers than we are to offer them.

How God Gives

To encourage us to ask God for wisdom, James gives us something wonderful—theology. He reminds us of what God is like. And he shows us just how beautifully God responds to our requests for help. We are reminded of what James' older brother, Jesus, taught about prayer: "If you, then, though you are evil, know how to give good gifts to your children, how much more will your Father in heaven give good gifts to those who ask him!" (Matthew 7:11).

This is what it means to have God as our Father. He is always poised to help. The key to asking God is knowing God. So savour the way in which God gives wisdom to those who ask him for it:

■ *He gives "generously"* (James **1:5**). God is not tight-fisted with his wisdom. I was at a buffet some time ago where the servers were giving out what seemed quite measly portions of food, given what they were charging for it. A small pile of rice with a sneeze of curry to go with it. No small number of people complained. But God is not stingy like that with his wisdom, giving only a tiny morsel to each person who asks. No, he is wonderfully generous. We need to take care not to think of him as cautious with his gifts, when in fact he delights to lavish them.

- *He gives to all* (**v 5**). God's wisdom is not something that is re-stricted to only a few privileged Christians. God intends it to be enjoyed and used by all his people. The Christian life is not a like one of those airline membership schemes where there are differ-ent tiers, and only the Platinum Members enjoy the good seats, while the rest are left to flounder. If you belong to God, his wis-dom, and all his wisdom, is for you.

- *He gives "without finding fault"* (**v 5**). When we come to our Father asking for wisdom in the middle of great turmoil, he is not shaking his head saying: *Man, you really messed all that up... Come on, don't you know by now how to handle this?* He is not tut-tutting as he guides and leads us.

Notice what James is doing here. He's reminding us of what we al-ready know about God. This is key. As we approach him in times of distress and confusion, we need to remind ourselves of who we know this God to be—of who he has shown himself to be.

These are truths we discovered when we first began to believe the message of the **gospel**. We realised then just how generous God is. We learned that he gave us no less than his one and only Son (John 3:16). That should give us great confidence in continuing to come to God with requests. "He who did not spare his own Son, but gave him up for us all—how will he not also, along with him, graciously give us all things?" (Romans 8:32). God's generosity does not dry up the moment we become a Christian. It continues to flow inexhaustibly into our lives.

When we first became a Christian, we also discovered how true it is that he gives to *all*. We had come to see something of the true state of our hearts and just how far from God we had wandered. Yet he was willing to give so freely, even to us—even people as flawed and warped as us. There really is no limit to his **grace**. We learned to think: *If he can be gracious to me, then no one is beyond his reach*.

And we saw how God gives without finding fault. That, in fact, *is* the gospel. We are given what we do not deserve, while the very faults that should disqualify us are wiped away. Through Christ we are presented faultless and blameless in his presence (Colossians 1:22).

This is the God we discovered when we first came to Christ. Why ever did we think he would have changed over the years? He loves his children. He longs to help us. He is utterly sincere in his desire to give us wisdom. He has become no less giving over the passing days. We can come to him! The sixteenth-century **Reformer** John Calvin summed this up brilliantly:

"Since we see that the Lord does not so require from us what is above our strength, but that he is ready to help us, provided we ask, let us, therefore, learn, whenever he commands anything, to ask of him the power to perform it."

(*Commentary on James*, page 282)

How We Ask

Having established God's generosity, what James says next comes as a bit of a shock. When we ask for wisdom, we "must believe and not doubt" (James **1:6**). It is not a small qualification that James has just introduced, and it might easily leave us reeling. Which Christian, after all, has not experienced doubt at some point? Does this mean that Christians who have doubted can now never have confidence when coming to God for wisdom?

There's a memorable scene towards the end of the movie *Indiana Jones and the Last Crusade* where Indy is looking for the Holy Grail so that he can save his father's life. He knows he is on the right path, but suddenly encounters a deep ravine. After a few moments' hesitation, he realises it is a test. He has to believe the way forward is somehow there for him. So he says to himself over and over again: "I must believe… I must believe…" Eventually, having psyched himself up, he steps out and finds a secret path, camouflaged by the darkness of the ravine.

Our fear as we come to these words in James' letter is that he means for us to do something similar—to work ourselves up into a state of absolute belief. Thankfully, this is not what James is talking about. He is using the word "doubt" in a very specific way here, and we need to see what he means (and doesn't mean) by it. James is not saying that we must never have had a spiritual question, or struggled to understand the ways of God, or wrestled with parts of the Bible's teaching. James is not saying we need to have worked ourselves up into a state of absolute belief.

As ever when studying what particular parts of the Bible mean, looking at the **context** is key. How James goes on to explain this verse helps us to see what particular kind of doubt he has in mind.

Doubt and Double-Mindedness

As James unpacks what he means by "doubt", it is immediately apparent that he's talking about someone who has split loyalties. By doubt, James means someone who is "double-minded" (**v 8**): someone we might think of as fickle or two-faced.

In other words, the doubter is someone who wants to hedge their bets two ways. They'll ask God for wisdom, but they'll also look over their shoulder to see if anyone has anything better on offer. They'll check out what the Bible says, but they'll also check out what the wisdom of the world says. They don't believe God's ways will necessarily and always be the best ways. They are double-minded: trying to live in more than one direction at once. They think they can switch between worldly wisdom and God's wisdom at will and get the best of both. Two foundations are better than one, right?

No, says James. In reality, this way of living makes you "unstable". I lived in Oxford for several years. In the summer months the city filled to bursting with tourists and visitors from around the globe. If you were lucky, you might see some of them attempting to use punts, the little wooden boats that crowd the rivers of the city, operated and steered by pushing a long pole into the water. Just getting onto a punt is something of an art. As you stand on the river bank, you lower one foot onto a small, rocking piece of wood, and it is not uncommon for the force of doing so to inadvertently push the punt away from the quayside. Many a hapless tourist has found themselves with one foot in the boat, the other on the bank, and their legs drifting quickly apart, briefly performing the splits before plunging into the water below.

Doing the splits when you're not expecting to is not a pleasant experience. Nor, says James, is the spiritual equivalent. The double-minded doubter, like the teetering would-be punter, is in a deeply precarious position. One foot is in the kingdom of God: the other in the world. Christian wisdom is pulling them in one direction: worldly wisdom in the other. They are unstable. James likens them to turbulent waves bouncing haphazardly all over the sea (**v 6**). With such a mindset, they will receive nothing from God (**v 7**).

> We need to be as sincere about receiving God's wisdom as he is about giving it to us.

James' point is clear. We need to be as sincere about receiving God's wisdom as he is about giving it to us.

If we are—if we genuinely seek to go God's way in a difficult time, trusting his way to be the right way—we can be assured that he will give wisdom to us. He promises to.

Understanding the Promise

This is not to say that we will always feel awash with wisdom. James is not saying that the moment we come to God, earnestly seeking his wisdom and guidance, we will experience a sudden flash of insight and feel as though we now know exactly what we need to do. I know of many Christians who have prayed for wisdom in the heat of a confusing crisis and felt none the wiser for having done so. The situation remained as confusing as before they prayed. What went wrong? Were they doubting?

There is a difference between receiving wisdom and feeling wise. It may well be that when we pray for wisdom, we feel none the wiser for having done so. But that is not the same as saying we have not received wisdom. **Verse 5** is a promise. When we ask with the sincerity of heart that James urges on us, "it will be given". This means that God's wisdom will direct us in the decisions we then go on to make. We may not feel any more confident, but God will protect us from folly. Whether or not we feel or perceive it at the time, God will have given us wisdom.

When we lack wisdom, as we often do in the heat of trials, we ask God, assured that he will give what we need to receive. That's the kind of God he is.

Questions for reflection

1. Which of the truths about how God gives on pages 18-19 particularly encouraged you?

2. Have you ever been, or are you in danger of being right now, a "double-minded" person? How did it feel to do the spiritual splits?

3. About what in your life do you need to ask for wisdom today? Will you do so?!

2. AGAINST PRIDE AND DECEPTION

No one likes a boaster—someone who self-confidently points to their own achievements or accumulations and demands praise for them. We try to teach our children not to do it. We're not normally impressed when people around us do it. We (hopefully) try to avoid it ourselves. And in the New Testament we are warned against it. To take one example: "Where, then, is boasting? It is excluded. Because of what law? The law that requires works? No, because of the 'law' that requires faith" (Romans 3:27). The gospel eradicates boasting. Being saved by faith gives us no basis for boasting—in fact, it completely undermines it. So we might be a little puzzled by what James asks us to do in these verses.

James is continuing to help his readers get from James 1:2 to **verse 12**: from experiencing trials to standing the test. So far he's **counselled** them to consider it pure joy (v 2-4) and to ask God for wisdom (v 5-8). But his next instruction involves doing what we've seen Paul ruling out: boasting (**v 9-11**)! These Christians are to "boast" in their position (**v 9**, ESV translation). But as we'll see, James has a very different kind of boasting in mind. This is not boasting that is contradicted by the gospel (boasting in ourselves), but boasting in the gospel (boasting in what God has done for us). Key to doing this is understanding what it will mean for those in contrasting economic circumstances: those who are poor and those who are wealthy.

At first glance, it looks as though James has suddenly jumped tracks. We've been talking about suffering and perseverance, and now we're suddenly talking about wealth: "Believers in humble circumstances ought to take pride in their high position. But the rich should take pride in their **humiliation**…" (**v 9-10**).

But James is not a scatterbrain who can't help switching from one subject to the next. The principle behind what he says to the rich and to the poor is the same in each case—they are to take pride in their position. As we think about what that means, we realise that he has not changed topic at all. James addresses these two groups of Christians at this point because our economic situation is not incidental to how we cope with trials. Christians are more affected by wealth (or lack of wealth) than we like to think. James' advice on this, coming at this very point, suggests that our outlook and reactions can be significantly swayed by where we find ourselves on the economic scale.

Whichever end of the pecking order we may happen to be at, his advice is the same: we are to boast in our position. Not in our financial position, but our spiritual position—the position we have before God: the position in which the gospel of Jesus Christ has placed us. This is a very different kind of boasting to what we normally see in the world around us. In fact, it is the gospel itself that prompts this, because it is the gospel itself that we are to boast in.

What that looks like is different for rich and poor. The same gospel affects us in different ways. The rich will have different blind spots and temptations to the poor. Each needs to see how the gospel applies particularly to them.

Enriching News for the Poor

James starts off addressing the poor: those in "humble circumstances" (**v 9**). Many of his readers will be in this situation. Elsewhere James makes reference to poor Christians being exploited by the rich (2:6). Some of their trials, at least, are economic.

To most societies, and especially in the west, to be poor is to be something of a failure at life. And so the poor are to strive for more; to dream of a better existence. They should aspire to becoming something greater. Endless adverts in the media tantalise us with images of success and wealth. The message is clear: *This is what you should most want.* The bigger house, the faster car, the more glamorous image, the more exotic travel. With wealth you can feel important. You have power. You are a somebody.

Though we might like to think otherwise, Christians are easily taken in by this message. We may know that this is not what life is about, and that all these things are not what we are designed to find satisfaction in. But it's so easy to find our minds wandering, and for us to start daydreaming about how much easier and more enjoyable things would be, if only we had a little bit more.

That is exactly where the gospel comes in. The message of the gospel to even the poorest and most destitute Christian is that in Christ, you are a somebody. However materially lacking life might be, James says the poor believers are to consider

> The message of the gospel to even the poorest Christian is that in Christ, you are a somebody.

their "high position" (**1:9**). This is what the gospel has given them. *Spiritually*, James tells them, *you have it made.* There is an incredible inheritance to look forward to. All that the Father has for his Son has been extended to those who are Christ's. It is an unfathomable prospect, and one that begins spiritually now with our standing before the Father in Christ.

Christians who are poor need reminding of this at any time, but especially in times of trial. James is urging his readers, when the world is looking down on them because of their circumstances, to remember that because of Christ they are spiritually rich. The tendency can easily be towards bitterness, especially if there are wealthier Christians around who are suffering less. They are instead to boast: to take great pride in the fact that in the sight of the only One who matters, they are as exalted as they could be. In Christ, they could not be more highly regarded by the Father. This is what they need consciously to remember in times of trial. The discipline to keep this perspective will help them to persevere and stand the test (**v 12**).

Humbling News for the Rich

The rich believers, by contrast, are to take pride in their low position (**v 10**).

Just as the world around us tends to think of the poor as something of a failure at life, it also tends to think of the wealthy as those who've made it and who can now revel in their success. To be wealthy is to have won the game, succeeded at life and fulfilled what it's all about. Rich people are to be admired and envied. Their lives and homes are splashed across magazines and feature articles, so that the rest of us know what we're missing out on. We love even a glimpse into what life is like for the wealthy. Everyone else perceives the rich as being problem-free. After all, they're rich! What more could they possibly want?!

It is a great temptation for the rich to be defined by their wealth— in their own eyes no less than in others'. Jesus himself talked about "the deceitfulness of wealth" (Mark 4:19). There is something intrinsically deceptive about wealth. It is all too easy for it to skew our view of ourselves and our abilities. The rich man walked away from Jesus empty-handed not because he didn't want salvation, but because he couldn't bear to *need* it (Mark 10:22).

Once again, we need to remember the way the gospel contradicts the assessment of the world around us. For the rich Christian, no matter how much wealth they have and how great their standing is in the eyes of the world, the gospel is deeply and irreversibly humbling. They have had to acknowledge before God that however rich they are materially, they are utterly bankrupt spiritually. They are only a Christian because God has been generous, not because of any of their own achievements or accumulations. Spiritually, they have what they have because God has shown them grace. They needed a spiritual handout. They've come to God for charity.

As well as this, James encourages the rich to remember just how fleeting acclaim can be: "They will pass away like a wild flower. For the sun rises with scorching heat and withers the plant; its blossom falls and its beauty is destroyed. In the same way, the rich will fade away even while they go about their business" (James **1:10-11**).

The rich person is a wild flower that quickly passes away. One of the great deceits of wealth is the impression it gives of solidity. It feels permanent and dependable, as if it can be counted on to bear the weight of our lives. We tend to equate wealth with security. Once we have enough financial resources squirrelled away, we know we're covered. Life can throw what it likes at us, but we have the protective cushion of our wealth. Money enables us to weather the storms… or so we think.

James' picture of choice for what wealth is like is not the foundation stone or sturdy pillar that buildings need to keep them up. It is the wild desert flower. In its prime, it is a thing of beauty. There is colour and delicacy. At times in the desert, the landscape is carpeted by wildflowers lending a colourful hue to an otherwise barren view. But their beauty is matched by their brevity. Once the sun reaches full height and blasts the land with a scorching wind, it is not long before the flowers are gone. The colours go, the life withers out of them, and nothing is left. One quick blast of middle-eastern sun, and the whole show is over.

Such is the way of things with wealth. Whatever it is we have an abundance of in this life—whatever it is the world around us celebrates in us—it can all disappear in the blink of an eye. It may be the vagaries of the economy. Many have gone to bed rich and woken up poor. The bank balance can go from black to red in a flash. Maybe it is our mortality. Many have gone to bed rich, and not woken up. Other

> Many have gone to bed rich, and woken up poor… or not woken up.

kinds of wealth are no more durable. Good looks quickly fade. Sporting and academic prowess are soon displaced by the next wave of talent coming through. Relationships that looked and felt so dependable can fall apart astonishingly fast.

Wealth is fleeting. Whatever riches we may have will one day pass away. They are the last thing we should take pride in. We should hold to them only very lightly. They will not last. For the wealthy to be defined by such riches is for them to "fade away even while they go about their business" (**v 11**), spiritually withering away even as they seem materially to flourish.

Instead, the rich should learn to boast in their humiliation. They are to delight in just how much the gospel has shown them their real need for dependence on God. Their boast is not to be in who they are and what they have, but in Jesus: what he has done, remembering exactly where they would be without him. It is a sign of good health indeed when a wealthy Christian enjoys reflecting on how they are nothing without Jesus; when they can laugh at the confidence the world might put in their assets and possessions, knowing themselves that the only thing of solidity and permanence in this world is the love of God shown in Christ.

This is especially needed in times of trial. When difficulties come, it is easy for the rich to think they can depend on themselves. Wealth makes people think that ability in the economic sphere translates into ability in the spiritual sphere. The gospel shows us it does not. We are not where the strength comes from: God is. He is the one who is able. And the only true wealth that counts is dependence on him. He is the only real and lasting treasure. Without him we are bankrupt, even with all the money in the world. The rich are not only to know that, but also to *boast* in that—to make it their badge of honour.

Persevere through Trials

In order to persevere through hardship, Christians are to take pride in their gospel position. Each of us needs to consider how this will work in our own lives. We need to think about our own circumstances—which of James' two categories we predominantly fit into. Do our circumstances tend to push us to feel shame or self-importance? It may be that we veer between the two, depending on the situation.

The poor are to remember their high position; they have been exalted by the gospel. The rich are to remember their low position; they have been humbled by the gospel. The poor need to reflect on the certainty of heaven; the rich on the transience of earth. It is God's estimation that counts, and it contradicts our own instinctive view of ourselves (itself largely shaped by our economic status).

The promise of James' **beatitude** can now come into view: "Blessed is the one who perseveres under trial because, having stood the test, that person will receive the crown of life that the Lord has promised to those who love him" (**v 12**).

It is as we learn to take pride in our gospel-given position that we are able to stand the test. It is doing this that is an expression of, and a vehicle for, our love for God. And as we continue to allow our view of ourselves to be shaped by the matchless worth of being made more like Christ, we can look forward with greater anticipation to the day when all trials will have come to an end, and when the only thing weighing us down will be the crown of life, which God will place on the heads of all who treasure him.

Questions for reflection

1. Are you in humble circumstances, or rich? (It may vary depending on where you are or who you are with.)

2. Given your previous answer, how might you forget the gospel and base your pride and confidence (or lack of it) on your circumstances?

3. What changes when you view yourself in terms of your gospel position? When will you next particularly need to remember to do this?

PART TWO

Don't Be Deceived

Some deceit is obvious. Just a cursory glance through the spam folder of the average email account will show emails from people claiming to be a bank, asking for confirmation of account details; from apparently generous friends in Nigeria offering to transfer several hundred thousand dollars to the recipient; from people offering financial loans at extraordinary rates; and many emails purporting to be from global celebrities like Oprah or Angelina demanding attention. The reason these are all in the spam folder is that they are easily identifiable as bogus emails.

But not all deceit is so obvious. There are scams all around us, in virtually every area of life. I recently saw a television show about people who had been swindled by companies claiming to offer good deals on home extensions and building projects, but which basically took the money and disappeared.

It is all too easy to be deceived in the Christian life as well—to think we are being attentive to God when we are not, and to think we are pleasing God with our lives when we are not. And to be deceived in this area matters more, and is noticed less, than financial swindles.

In the next few verses James warns us a number of times not to be deceived:

- "Don't be deceived, my dear brothers and sisters" (**v 16**).

- "Do not merely listen to the word, and so deceive yourselves" (v 22).

- "Those who consider themselves religious and yet do not keep a tight rein on their tongues deceive themselves, and their religion is worthless" (v 26).

And James begins by warning us about being deceived in the whole area of temptation.

Once again, we may think James is abruptly switching topics. He's talked for a while about how we respond to trials and now he's moved on to the topic of temptation. But these two issues are closely related. So far, James has been concerned with how we respond to the difficult external circumstances around us. Now he turns his attention to what goes on within us at such times. In fact, the Greek word for "test" in **verse 12** (*peirazo*) is the same word translated as "tempt" in **verses 13-14**. The two often go together. Trials around us can prompt all manner of temptations within us. Understanding temptation is therefore vital for ensuring that we respond in healthy ways to the difficult circumstances we often find ourselves in. As New Testament scholar Douglas Moo writes:

> "No solid line should be drawn between **v 12** and **v 13**, as if James is dropping the topic of testing to take up the issue of temptation. His concern, rather, is to help his readers resist the temptation that comes along with the trial." (*James*, page 72)

And as we consider temptation, we need to make sure we are not deceived. So James needs to tell us a few home truths about ourselves (**v 13-15**), along with some essential truths about God (**v 16-18**).

Know Yourself

James begins by encouraging us to take a look at ourselves: "When tempted, no one should say, 'God is tempting me.' For God cannot be tempted by evil, nor does he tempt anyone" (**v 13**).

We are to expect temptation. James says: "When tempted..." He does not say: *Now, if you happen to be tempted...* or: *If you're one of those particularly weak Christians who experiences temptation...* James expects temptation to be a normal feature in the Christian life. There are times when Christians are particularly conscious of temptation. There can be periods when it is unusually intense, or when we find ourselves especially disturbed by what tempts us. Equally, there are other times when it is easy not even to notice temptation—and these times are more spiritually dangerous. Temptations come, and we fail even to spot what is happening until we have given into them and sinned.

You are going to be tempted. You may well be experiencing temptation right now. Temptation is our constant companion, from cradle to grave. And so we need not to be surprised by temptation, and we do need to understand it.

Where Temptation Comes From

Our reflex so often is to lay the blame for our temptation elsewhere. This is a tendency that runs very deep in us, and we find it very easy to blame God for the temptations we experience. We might find ourselves thinking: *God is the one who made me like this. He's the one who gave me this weakness. He's the one who put me in this situation.*

But James counters this by reminding us of what God is like: "God cannot be tempted by evil" (**v 13**). He is un-tempt-able. Sin holds no attraction to him, as it does to us. He is utterly pure. And because of this, we can be sure that he is not trying to trip us up, looking for ever more inventive ways to tempt us into sin. God is not to blame for our temptation: we are. And notice this is the case for every single one of us: "Each person is tempted when they are dragged away by their own evil desire and enticed" (**v 14**).

The uncomfortable truth is this: the evil desire tugging away at us *is our own*. We can't blame any of the things around us. It is not the fault of our parents, our peers, our circumstances, our genes or our God.

The American pastor Tim Keller has likened this to failing an exam. I once spectacularly failed a school chemistry exam. I got 11%, and suspect most of that was just for getting my name right. But I can't blame my failure on the teacher for setting the exam. It was my fault—I'd done virtually no work for it, and the exam showed that up. We'd been taught the material in class, and were given plenty of notice that the exam was coming up, and ample time to prepare and revise. The exam was the occasion for my failure, but it was not the cause of it. And the same is true when it comes to temptation and sin. My circumstances may be the occasion for my sin, but they are not the cause of it.

No, our own desires are the cause of temptation. The desire to sin that wells up within us comes from our own hearts. Temptation would not be tempting if I were pure and not evil. This is reinforced by what James tells us about how temptation works.

How Temptation Works

James describes how we are dragged away by our temptations and enticed (**v 14**). It is the language of a hunt, of luring and coaxing the prey into the open and then striking, killing and dragging it away to be devoured. We think of those predators that are able to make themselves attractive to their victim, so that it actually delivers itself up for the taking. This is how our own desires work against us.

James is showing us something deeply profound about our human nature, for we are both agent and victim of our desires. The desires are our own, from our own hearts—yet it is us that they entice and attack. Within each of us there is this deep tension. We really are our own worst enemies.

Where Temptation Leads

James shows us the result of temptation; notice where it all leads: "Then, after desire has conceived, it gives birth to sin; and sin, when it is full-grown, gives birth to death" (**v 15**).

James describes the process in terms of two births. Births are normally occasions for great celebration; but not in this case.

Desire gives birth to sin. Our desires, when fed and nurtured in our hearts and minds, inevitably lead to action. When those desires are ungodly, so too is the resulting behaviour. Sin is born. And once born, it does what babies do—it grows stronger. We like to think that giving in to sin is a way of "getting it out of our system"; that if we indulge it, it'll go away and leave us alone. James shows us just how mistaken that thinking is. Acting on sin is never the end of it. It takes on a life of its own.

A friend of mine recently told me that his teenage son had beaten him in an arm wrestle for the first time. It was something of a turning point. Even though my friend himself is strong, he now knew his son was even stronger. James says it is the same with sin. Once it has been given birth, it grows until it reaches the point where we can no longer control it. It doesn't stop where we want it to and planned for it to. It keeps taking us further and further. And so we find ourselves doing things we never would have imagined.

> Sin doesn't stop where we want it to. It keeps taking us further.

But even that is not the end of it. Sin now gives birth to death (**v 15**). It is a grisly image, but it reminds us of where sin ultimately leads. Sin leads to death. This has always been the case. Back in the Garden of Eden God had warned the first human, Adam, that rebellion would mean "you will certainly die" (Genesis 2:17). And so it did, and so it does.

James wants us to see that all this starts with our desires. At the time, temptation feels so harmless. It feels as if it's on our side. It seems so warm and pleasant. But James has shown us where it all leads, so that we will learn that we need to fight sin at its conception. Bishop J.C. Ryle, writing in the late nineteenth century, wrote:

> "Habits, like trees, are strengthened by age. A boy may bend an oak when it is a sapling—a hundred men cannot root it up, when it is a full-grown tree." (*Thoughts For Young Men*, page 7)

In times of trial and temptation, it is all too easy to forget what we are truly like. We must take responsibility for the desires lurking in our hearts. James therefore warns us: "Don't be deceived, my dear brothers and sisters" (James **1:16**). It is self-deception that makes us so quick to blame God and excuse ourselves when we are tempted.

Knowing God

If one tendency is to forget how bad we are, another is to forget how good God is. In times of trial especially, we lose sight of the good things that God has given us. We can be deceived about what God is like. So, having reminded us of the evil desires that spring up from within, James now draws our attention to the good gifts that come down from above: "Every good and perfect gift is from above, coming down from the Father of the heavenly lights, who does not change like shifting shadows" (**v 17**).

God is the source of all blessing, and James describes him in a number of wonderful terms.

- *Sovereign: The Father of heavenly lights.* God is the Creator. He is the one who made the stars and fixed them in place. He charts their course. He is the cosmic and glorious God, for whom all things are possible: the one who reigns over every corner of his universe. And it is *this* Creator God who wonderfully takes an interest in us. This God loves us and knows us, and gives great gifts to us.

- *Dependable: The God who does not change.* God made the stars, but he is unlike them in an important way. Like the heavenly lights, our own planet is constantly moving. The whole universe is a swirl of motion. As a result, shadows are never still but continuously shifting. Yesterday I had the opportunity to sit outside in the sunshine to do some reading. But it wasn't long before I had to move. I was being chased round the garden by the shadow of a large tree nearby. Added to that were the large clouds scudding overhead, plunging the garden into periods of gloom.

  All this motion is a reflection of God's creative power. But though God made the heavenly lights, he is not like them. Where they are constantly moving, he is unchanging and constant. He is not forever shifting his position. In Christ, we have found the perfect spot to bask in his grace, and we never need to move. God is not fickle. He does not go through phases. We are not flavour of the month for a time and then cast aside and forgotten about. God is always good to us, and his commitment to us never falters.

■ *Gracious: The God who gives us new birth.* James has already shown us a cycle of birth—the grim births of sin and death. It is the natural order of things. The only answer to that cycle is a new one. And it is this new cycle that now defines those who have come to Christ: "He chose to give us birth through the word of truth, that we might be a kind of firstfruits of all he created" (**v 18**).

James tells us a number of important things about this new birth:

- *Its origin:* It has been given to us. It comes as a gracious gift from God. It is not something we have somehow earned; he "chose" to give it to us.

- *Its means:* This new birth has come by the "word of truth". The births of sin and death came as a result of our listening to our evil desires; this has come through our coming under the word of God. So powerful is the message of Jesus that it can penetrate us, grip us, and make us into new people.

- *Its result:* The effect of this birth is that we become like firstfruits of God's creation. Our earlier cycle of birth had brought about death; this now brings life. The firstfruits are the initial batch of a farmer's crop that proves and guarantees the rest of the harvest is now on its way. Our new life is just the beginning of what God is up to, a plan that incorporates the whole of creation as renewal finally comes to all things.

James reminds us that every perfect gift comes from above, from God's gracious hand. But there is none so wonderful as this gift of new birth in our hearts. It is to this that James points when reminding us that God is powerfully, dependably and graciously good. And it's this that we need to keep in the forefronts of our minds, especially when facing the trials and temptations that will be a part of our lives each day.

Questions for reflection

1. What temptations are you regularly battling (or giving in to) at the moment?

2. Has this chapter changed how you view those temptations? How?

3. How does the description of God in verses 17-18 motivate you to resist those temptations? How does it reassure you when you fail?

3. MORE THAN LISTENING

There are times when it really matters how well we listen. I have developed the bad habit, when occasionally chatting with friends or family on the phone, of doing other things at the same time, like surfing the net or checking email.

Usually I can get away with half-listening, but there are times when listening carefully is incredibly important. A few years ago, I needed to have some major surgery on my intestine. Before the operation, I sat down with the surgeon and he talked me through what he was about to do and what would happen as a result. Needless to say, I absorbed every word he spoke with great care.

Every time we open the Bible, it matters that we listen well. Fundamental to what we know about God is that he speaks. It is not an incidental activity. He created the universe by his words (Hebrews 11:3, ESV), and now brings new spiritual life to his people by that same means. We have just seen in James how God has chosen to give us new birth "through the word of truth" (James 1:18). God relates to us through his word.

We therefore need to be people who listen properly to what God says. It is another of the areas where James is showing us we can be easily deceived: "Do not merely listen to the word, and so deceive yourselves. Do what it says" (**v 22**). The awful danger is that we can think we're responding in the right way to God's word when, in fact, we are not.

So how do we listen properly to God? In a nutshell, to listen to God rightly we need not only to hear his word, but also to accept it and obey it.

Good Listener?

James says: "My dear brothers and sisters, take note of this: everyone should be quick to listen, slow to speak and slow to become angry" (**v 19**). It sounds like classic, timeless advice—the sort of thing you might see on an inspirational desk calendar. It is good advice for anyone. But James is not making a public-service announcement; he is writing to help Christians wholeheartedly live out their faith.

In particular, James is mindful of how many of his readers are facing trials of many kinds (v 2), and this is particularly important advice for those who are suffering. It is in times of severe hardship that we can be much slower to listen, and quicker to speak. We can become consumed by what we are going through—it is sometimes all we can think about and therefore all we are likely to want to talk about. We listen less to what others are saying; our own experience and take on what is going on drowns out everything else.

James also relates this tendency to anger. When our listening slows, it is not only our speaking that can quicken, but also our temper. Such anger is not pleasing to God "because human anger does not produce the righteousness that God desires" (**v 20**). What we do with words, both those we speak and those spoken to us, greatly affects the way we live.

Jesus himself is a wonderful example for us in this regard. The gospel writers do not hide the fact that he was angry on occasion. At times it was because of the pompous behaviour of his disciples (eg: Mark 10:14), or the callous attitude of the religious leaders (eg: Mark 3:5). When he cleared the temple, it was because it looked more like a shopping mall than a house of prayer (Mark 11:15-17). On such occasions, Jesus was right to be angry. We know that such anger was justified, and we know that it was slow in coming.

Too often, our anger is neither of those things. Think about the last couple of times you lost your temper. How quickly did it happen? What caused it? We can easily be angry at the wrong things and in the wrong way; our anger can be quick and misdirected. The teaching of James and the example of Jesus provide an important corrective.

James broadens things out in the next verse: "Therefore, get rid of all moral filth and the evil that is so prevalent, and humbly accept the word planted in you, which can save you" (James **1:21**). We need to be ruthless with our sin. We can so easily become covered with moral filth, because it is all around us.

Once again, James is not jumping around between different subjects—listening advice, anger-management, and now **ethics**. All these things are bound up with one underlying issue: how we respond to God's word. The way we rid ourselves of sin is by humbly accepting God's word (**v 21**). If you want to have a better heart, a more godly mind, a cleaner mouth and more productive hands, make sure you use your ears. We are not going to change without God's word. It is when we have learned to listen carefully to him that we can begin to live lives that please him.

> If you want a better heart, make sure you use your ears.

This is the case for any relationship. To know how to please someone, you need to have listened to them for long enough to know what it is they like. The people who are hardest to buy Christmas presents for are the friends or relatives that you don't know very well. Why? Because you have less of an idea of what they're into. You need to spend time with someone if you are ever to develop a sense of what they like.

Occasionally after a church service, while I'm out in the church foyer chatting to people as they leave, someone will come and bring me a coffee. It is a lovely gesture; they are wanting to do something nice for me. The problem is I can't stand coffee, and so I'll either awkwardly accept it and then discreetly pass it on to somebody else, or I'll thank them profusely while explaining that I don't drink the stuff. Those who know me well know to bring me just a mug of hot water!

The way to rid ourselves of moral filth, and instead to produce the righteousness that God desires and which pleases him, is to accept his word. All of which raises a very important question: what place are we giving to the word of God in our lives? Are we listening?

There are two important disciplines that Christians have cultivated over the years to help them to listen to God's word.

1. Studying the Bible with Others

Christians have always instinctively understood listening to God to be a corporate activity. After he was raised from the dead, Jesus looked at the Scriptures with two of his disciples, who later reported how their hearts burned within them as Jesus explained the true meaning of the texts they studied with him (Luke 24:27, 32). From its earliest days, the church in Acts devoted itself to the teaching of the apostles (Acts 2:42). In Berea, the Jews were commended as an example of receiving the gospel message enthusiastically, and then earnestly searching the Scriptures daily to see if Paul's teaching was true. We are told that as a result of this, "many of them believed" (Acts 17:11-12). Later in life, Paul impressed upon Timothy the centrality of preaching the word of God and of handling it correctly (2 Timothy 4:1-2; 2:15). God's word has always been at the centre of the corporate life of his people.

It is for this reason that, in addition to the public teaching of God's word in services, many churches encourage their members to study the Bible together regularly in smaller groups. These are a wonderful way for a group of Christians to learn from and teach one another together. One of the highlights of my week is studying the Bible with colleagues on a Monday lunchtime. Almost without exception, we will learn things from having examined the passage together that we never would have learned if we were looking at it on our own. It is a precious time of the week.

2. Studying the Bible on our Own

We must not lose the corporate aspect of listening to God's word, but nor must we allow this to be the only way we come into contact with the Bible. Just as vital as looking at the Scriptures with others is cultivating the discipline of looking at it on our own. In various Christian traditions this has become known as the "quiet time", a period set aside each day to read and reflect on a passage of Scripture and to spend time in private prayer. It is no accident that earlier generations referred to it as a Christian's "devotional life", for it is not merely an exercise in personal instruction but, above all else, a means of deepening your relationship with God. Many have found first thing in the morning the best time to do this. How vital for God's word to be the first voice we hear each day before our mind is crowded out with the matters of the coming 24 hours! Others have found lunch breaks or during a long commute to be the most practical time. But what matters more than when and where we look at God's word is that we actually do it. Those who have never done so, or have fallen out of the habit, would do well to think carefully about how they might set about starting afresh.

Quick to Listen

We need to accept God's word. And there is no way to do this that is not going to take some time. It involves thought and consideration.

I recently watched the Academy Awards on TV. The tendency of those receiving Oscars is to offer fulsome thanks to all and sundry, and so one of the challenges organisers face each year is how to keep these acceptance speeches to time and prevent the whole show overrunning. The general strategy was to allow an allotted time for each recipient, and at the end of this allotted time, irrespective of whether they had finished proffering thanks or were just getting warmed up (and were only as far as thanking the teacher they had when they were six), the orchestra struck up and played them off. Even a Hollywood star knows they can't compete with a 70-piece orchestra at full blast.

And there is a danger that this is how we treat God. We do want to listen to him, to get to know the Bible, and for his word to change us. But when we finally get round to opening our Bibles, it can be as if we're saying to God: *Lord, please speak to me. And you've got 60 seconds / five minutes / till my train reaches its stop.* Anything longer than that, and we'll mentally play him off the stage and get under way with the next thing on the day's agenda.

It matters how we listen, and nowhere is that more true than when it is God we are listening to. James began by teaching us that we needed to be "quick to listen" and "slow to speak" (James **1:19**). In fact, he told us to "take note of" it. It is something that needs to be jotted down on a mental post-it note and stuck right at the forefront of our minds. It is good advice for anyone, in pretty much any situation. It is the stuff of worldly wisdom: "You've got two ears and one mouth: remember why!" But it is especially wise when we apply it to our relationship with God. There, more than anywhere else, we need to be quicker to listen and slower to speak. James is not commending silence; he has much to say in this letter about prayer. But he is challenging us to be listeners first. It is all too easy to reel off before God all that we are experiencing and needing, especially when we are encountering trials. Yet what we most need is the wisdom that only God can give (v 5). And that wisdom lies in his word, first and foremost. If we truly wish to be wise, we need humbly to accept the word God has so kindly planted in us and written down for us.

> In our relationship with God, we are to be listeners first.

Questions for reflection

1. What kind of listener of God's word are you? Can you think of recent examples in your own life where you have listened well to the Lord?

2. "Everyone should be quick to listen, slow to speak and slow to become angry" (v 20). In what situations do you find one (or more) of these commands especially difficult?

3. Do you need to see God's word differently, or make practical changes, in order to become a better listener?

PART TWO

Don't Only Listen

If one problem is that we don't listen to the word of God, another is that we often *only* listen, and do nothing more than that. Listening alone is not enough: "Do not merely listen to the word, and so deceive yourselves. Do what it says" (**v 22**).

The word of God needs to be obeyed by the child of God. The word has been planted in us (**v 21**) but that does not mean our role is now passive. It is not that we now just sit back and do nothing while the word automatically grows in our lives and does its thing. We need to "do what it says". Listening is vital, but merely listening is just as foolish as not listening.

James underlines this with a snapshot from everyday life. How we should approach the word is a little like how we should approach a mirror. Whenever we look at the word, we are like "someone who looks at his face in a mirror" (**v 23**). What truly matters is not the look we take, but the action we take as a result of the look.

The Importance of Obedience

There have been countless times when I've been about to head out into the day and I've glanced at myself in the mirror only to discover that, presentation-wise, I am a bit of a disaster. There is a blob of ketchup on my shirt, or my sweater is on inside out, or my tie is dramatically askew, or my top is displaying a visual record of everything I've eaten in the last 12 hours.

What do I do next, having seen the issues? I rectify them. The clothing is dabbed; the jumper reapplied more carefully; the tie straightened up; or the top changed.

This is why we use mirrors. They show us a problem, so that we can sort it out straight away. What we generally don't do, or at least should never do, is what the character in James' little **parable** does:

nothing. It is foolish to be someone who "goes away" from the mirror "and immediately forgets what he looks like" (**v 24**). Having realised that we look a public embarrassment, we don't then ignore that fact. Otherwise, there really was no point in looking at the mirror in the first place.

James' point here is not complicated. God's word is to have the same kind of effect on us as a mirror. We are supposed to act on what it shows us right away. Like a mirror, God's word shows us what we are really like. Elsewhere in the New Testament, God's word is described as a double-edged sword (Hebrews 4:12). As we read it, it cuts back on us. It challenges, provokes and confronts us. It reads us. Whenever you read your Bible, one of the things that happens is that it shows you *you*.

> Whenever you read your Bible, it shows you *you*.

This has been the experience of millions of Christians. I know one woman who started reading the Gospel of Mark because her younger brother had recently become a Christian, and she wanted to understand what it was he was now getting himself into. It was purely an exercise in gaining some information. But it was not long before she discovered Mark's Gospel was actually reading her. Much as she tried, she could not just keep it at arm's length. She said she felt as though it was scrutinising and exposing her. It was laying bare her heart and her motives. She was seeing truths about herself she had never known. She began to realise what it meant to have turned from God in her life. Not long after, she became a Christian. The Bible, she discovered, was just like a mirror. And she acted on what she saw of herself.

This is how it is designed to be for all Christians. It is not enough to listen to God's word. It is not enough to "get" what it says, or what a given passage might mean. A clever **cross-reference** may impress us, but it is not the same as obedience. We need to respond to it, to live in the light of it. To listen without responding to it is to walk out into the day ignoring the toothpaste that you just discovered is all across your face. If God's word does not have an impact on us, we are missing the point of reading it.

The Motivation for Obedience

But why bother? Obedience is always an effort, and often costly. So what will keep us resolved to "do what it says" as we read God's word (James **1:22**)? Again, James' point is straightforward: if we obey God's word we will be blessed. "Whoever looks intently into the perfect law that gives freedom and continues in it—not forgetting what they have heard but doing it—they will be blessed in what they do" (**v 25**).

Notice James is not merely saying that obedient Christians will be blessed in the future at the end of time. They will be blessed "in what they do". This blessing is enjoyed during life *now*.

What does that mean? We see something of what this means in the verse itself. James describes God's word in a number of ways in this chapter. It is the "word of truth", which gives us birth (v 18); it is the "word planted" in us, which we need to accept (**v 21**); and here, it is "the perfect law that gives freedom" (**v 25**).

James refers to it as "law". There are many different kinds of writing in the Bible. Many parts take the form of direct commands that need to be obeyed. There are many other parts that take the form of narrative, or poetry, or song. But by referring to God's word in general as "law", James is reminding us that all of it is calling us to do something. Every part of it, whatever its genre and form, demands a response of repentance and faith. We can never read it and just say: *Huh. That doesn't really speak into my life right now*. All of it is intended to change us, today. We need to think and pray carefully about how any section of Scripture applies to us. It is good to ask of any passage: "How should this affect my thinking? My attitude? My behaviour?"

But it is no burdensome law. It is "the perfect law that gives freedom". God's word is perfect. It is exactly what we need; it fits us perfectly. As we live by it, obeying its teaching, we discover freedom.

The Freedom of Obedience

Such a line of reasoning—*Obey all of God's word, and you'll be, and feel, free*—sounds absurd to many people today. The idea that a law (of all things) can lead to freedom seems laughable. But that is because we have misunderstood what freedom is.

Western society tends to think of freedom purely in terms of the absence of restriction. The idea is that if we remove all constraints, we end up with freedom. So the imposition of rules and boundaries is a restriction of freedom, by definition. But in the Bible, real freedom is not the absence of any and every constraint, but rather, the presence of the right kind of constraint. Removing a fish from water does not give it more freedom, but less. It is designed to live in the water, not apart from it. Freedom from water is a removal of constraint, but it is also (for a fish) a complete misunderstanding of what freedom really is.

Our own true freedom is only found when we are in the environment which we were designed to flourish in. And that is obedience to God's word. As we live by God's word, we experience true life. Only then can we be said to be properly free. God made us. As we follow his word and live in his ways, our lives end up going along the grain of how he has designed us to live. His word corresponds exactly to our nature.

All of this means that obedience should never be something we resent. Every command God gives us is for our good. In the Old Testament, King David could go so far as to say that the "commands of the Lord are radiant, giving light to the eyes" (Psalm 19:8). For most of us, encountering commands is not something we tend to associate with radiance. When we're driving and suddenly come across some speed restrictions, or when we're at work and our boss gives us a pile of tasks to do, we do not normally smile with delight. But it is different when it comes to God's commands, precisely because they are *God's*. The difference between his commands and anybody else's is that his are given purely out of love for us, and a desire for us to flourish and prosper.

Life is never better without God's word, and it is never poorer with it. No command will ever work against us if we follow it, and ignoring one will never actually end up being better for us. We must be careful not to misdefine freedom, and so disobey the very words that will bring us true freedom.

The Evidence of Obedience

Obedience to God's word is never simply mandated, nor vaguely beneficial. It is transformational. Following God's word changes us. Certain things will follow. Obedience will make a difference; and as James shows us just what that difference is, he gives us examples of some of the changes that will come. The presence or absence of these changes indicates whether or not we practise what James calls "true religion".

He begins with the negative—what true religion is not: "Those who consider themselves religious and yet do not keep a tight rein on their tongues deceive themselves, and their religion is worthless" (James **1:26**). James has already warned us that if we only listen to God's word and do nothing more, we deceive ourselves. Now he adds that if we do not keep a tight rein on our speech, we are similarly duped. This is a stark truth. Not controlling our speech is a sign that we are not actually following God. If we consider ourselves to be spiritual (or "Christian", or "religious") but are not keeping our words in check, then we are deluded. If we find ourselves to be saying things that are destructive, or untrue, or which get us into trouble and which we wish we'd never said, it may well be that we are not converted. James expects that Christians will have a measure of control over what they say. And this is quite sobering. It destroys the natural complacency we often fall into.

God's word teaches us that we should not gossip, or lie, or curse others (Colossians 3:8-9). It says there should be no obscenity or coarse joking (Ephesians 5:4). If these things are in any way a fixture of our speech, then we are kidding ourselves if we imagine that all is well between us and God.

Pure and Faultless Religion

Having dealt with the negative, James now comes to the positive: "Religion that God our Father accepts as pure and faultless is this: to look after orphans and widows in their distress and to keep oneself from being polluted by the world" (James **1:27**).

The proof that we truly listen and respond to God's word is seen in the presence of certain "determinations" in our life. We will be determined to care for the needy. The orphan and widow in James' day were the most destitute and vulnerable. There was no state provision for those who were unable to provide for themselves. Orphans and widows had no means of their own to make an income. They were emblematic of the most needy in society, as Douglas Moo points out:

"In the ancient world, with an absence of money-making possibilities for women and any kind of social welfare, widows and orphans were helpless to provide for themselves."

(*James*, page 97)

James says the true Christian will have a concern to help and provide for them. Their distress will matter to us. We will not be calloused to it, but responsive. God himself, after all, expresses his fatherhood in caring for the helpless (Psalm 68:5).

This may well be a challenging verse for those of us from more conservative churches. We are right to care about truth and sound doctrine. That is a key outworking of accepting God's word. We should make sure we understand it clearly. But there is a danger that we make such understanding an end in itself, rather than a means to the greater end of becoming more like our God in how we look after those in especial need. We can have no assurance that we really have received God's truth until such care is evidenced in our lives.

Further evidence of our true obedience to God is seen in a determination to avoid the moral pollution of the world. We might think of any number of ways in which the culture of the world around us is pushing in an opposite direction to the way that God has called us to live. But it is likely James has a particular form of pollution in mind. In the Greek, there is no "and" between these two characteristics of true religion. The verse literally reads: "to look after orphans and widows in their distress, to keep oneself from being polluted by the world". So the pollution James has in his mind is primarily economic exploitation and indifference. That James follows **1:27** with an immediate example of economic favouritism (2:1-13) further suggests this is the particular form of pollution he has in mind.

> The pollution James has in mind is primarily economic indifference.

The tongue, helping the impoverished, and in doing so not following the crooked thinking of the world—these are huge issues that James has raised. But he does not leave them here. Each of these topics forms what the bulk of the rest of the letter is about. Chapter 2 is primarily concerned with our attitude to the poor; chapter 3 with our use of the tongue, and the damage it can wreak when not kept under a tight rein; and chapter 4 unpacks more about what it means to be worldly in our thinking and behaviour.

In all that James says, we need to listen. And more than that, accept and obey the word God has for us. This is the way of true religion, and where true religion begins and flows from. This will be the way of freedom and blessing.

Questions for reflection

1. Do you ever confuse knowledge of God's word with obedience to God's word?

2. "We can have no assurance that we really have received God's truth until such care is evidenced in our lives." Does this reassure you, or challenge you, or both?

3. How have you experienced obedience leading to blessing and freedom in your own life? How could you use that past experience to encourage present obedience?

4. NO FAVOURITISM

James begins with a blunt command: "My brothers and sisters, believers in our glorious Lord Jesus Christ must not show favouritism" (**2:1**).

This is clearly not a **hypothetical** problem. James' directness suggests favouritism is a big issue among his readers. He gives them an example of the kind of thing he is talking about, and it is clearly not unheard of in the kind of churches James is writing to. A man turns up to church wearing "a gold ring and fine clothes"; at the same time, a poor man "in filthy old clothes" enters (**v 2**). Now, says James, "if you show special attention to the man wearing fine clothes and say, 'Here is a good seat for you,' but say to the poor man, 'You stand there' or 'Sit on the floor by my feet'" (**v 3**), what is happening? James answers: "Have you not discriminated among yourselves and become judges with evil thoughts?" (**v 4**).

It may be helpful to translate this scenario into a modern-day setting. It is Sunday morning at church, a few minutes before the service is due to start, and folk are arriving. Among them are two newcomers. The first is very wealthy and it is obvious. His suit has been tailor-made for him on Savile Row in London. He has a Rolex watch on his wrist. He has a golfing tan and smells pleasantly of plush aftershave. Some of the church members even recognise him—maybe he is a well known TV personality, or perhaps a local entrepreneur, or senior politician.

The second newcomer also arrives and could not be more different. He is very poor, and again it is immediately obvious. People can actually smell him before they can see him; he hasn't washed properly for weeks. And he looks a mess: his clothes are dirty, do not fit and are falling apart.

The two men are now in the building, and the welcomers are on them like a shot. To the first man, they gush: "Thank you so much for coming along this morning. It really is wonderful to have you with us. Please do come and take a seat with the congregation. If you sit in that section near the front, you'll be sure to have a good view of everything going on." They hand him the bulletin with the order of service and make sure he knows where everything is.

To the second man, they take a very different approach. First, they try to ignore him. Maybe he won't stay when he sees that he doesn't really fit in. They are very suspicious of why he would come to church. What does he want? Eventually, one of them, holding his breath, walks over and quietly says to him: "If you're going to stay in here during the service—and you might not want to—well, please stand over there at the back, out of everyone's way. We don't really want you causing any disruption." It quickly becomes apparent that this man has a bad leg; he is hobbling along in considerable pain. So one of the welcomers intercepts him: "OK, if you really must sit, then sit over there at the side, out of everyone's way."

Both men are new, and yet they are treated completely differently. One is welcomed, the other barely tolerated. The wealthy man is treated as if he is of much greater worth than the poor man. Clearly this sort of thing was not unheard of in James' day.

Attitude Problem

It is easy for us to react to a scenario like that in disgust. Most of us would never dream of behaving like that (or so we think). Certainly our welcome team at church know far better than to do things in that way. We might have our faults, but generally we are a welcoming bunch. This sort of thing would never happen. Maybe we can skip straight to the next chapter; this sort of thing really isn't an issue for us.

But... I have heard of good, Bible-teaching churches where committed, mature members suggested that a local homeless man should not be invited in, for fear that some of the regulars might be put off coming. And even if we can legitimately say this kind of thing has not happened, and could not happen, in our church, the issue James is highlighting goes far, far deeper than what we do with someone when they walk through the church door.

The kind of favouritism James is talking about reflects a particular attitude we can all have to people, and the example he has given us is just one expression of it. If this issue was a danger for Christians in his day, we can be very sure it's a danger in our own day too. Circumstances may have changed in all sorts of ways since James wrote his letter, but human nature is still very much the same.

James' point is a simple one: favouritism is profoundly un-Christian. It says, in effect, that someone who is worth more to the world is worth more to the church, and, correspondingly, that someone who is worth less to the world is worth less to the church. Favouritism ends up judging one person's soul as being of greater value than another's, and it does all this on the basis of superficial, worldly criteria.

> Acceptable religion is inclined *toward* the needy, not away from them.

James will have none of it. Such behaviour he describes as becoming "judges with evil thoughts" (**v 4**). His language is strong and uncompromising. Favouritism is not just to be frowned upon or gently discouraged; it is evil. In fact, it contradicts the very marks of authentic religion that James has just outlined at the end of chapter 1:

> "Religion that God our Father accepts as pure and faultless is this: to look after orphans and widows in their distress and to keep oneself from being polluted by the world." (1:27)

True and acceptable religion is actually inclined *toward* the needy, not away from them. Favouritism of the sort James has been describing is the opposite of not being polluted by the world: it is letting the world determine how much spiritual worth someone has based on their economic standing (or any other measure). It is a way of thinking that Christians can slip into all too easily. Churches need to take great care not to think of a wealthy unbeliever as being more important or worthy of ministry than a poor unbeliever, or to make a great fuss over someone important and powerful that we would never make over someone who is marginal, or to be far more excited about a celebrity coming into church one day than a homeless person.

Why Favouritism Opposes the Gospel

Because such thinking is so ingrained in our culture, it is likely we are far more influenced by it than we might like to think. In the next few verses James shows us why favouritism is to have no part in the Christian life.

To start with, it goes right against the grain of how God works. James invites his readers to look at the churches around them: "Has not God chosen those who are poor in the eyes of the world to be rich in faith and to inherit the kingdom he promised those who love him?" (**2:5**). The overwhelming majority of Christians at that time were from poorer backgrounds. Churches were not exactly rammed full of the well-to-do and influential. It was the opposite. James is asking his readers to look at the sort of people who are responding to the gospel; God is calling many who are poor.

Paul made a similar observation, writing not long after James:

"Brothers and sisters, think of what you were when you were called. Not many of you were wise by human standards; not many were influential; not many were of noble birth. But God chose the foolish things of the world to shame the wise; God chose the weak things of the world to shame the strong." (1 Corinthians 1:26-27)

We must not overstate the point. Neither James nor Paul is saying that the church is *only* full of the poor and weak, or that the wealthy and influential are not worth trying to reach. But both are pointing to a clear pattern. It is not random. God is choosing and calling people to himself in a particular way, and a striking feature of it is his propensity to do so from among the poor and lowly.

The same pattern is very much in evidence today. Globally, the church is overwhelmingly poor. Many of the places where the gospel is advancing the fastest are poor. Take the recent explosion of the evangelical church in Latin America, or in parts of Southeast Asia. Then and now, this pattern is hard to miss.

And we must notice what God is choosing them for: "to be rich in faith and to inherit the kingdom he promised those who love him" (James **2:5**). God has chosen the poor to have great spiritual riches—in Jesus, they've hit the jackpot. And with it comes wonderful spiritual dignity: they stand to inherit God's kingdom. They are heirs and princes. The world has given them the lowest of positions; God has given them the highest (as we saw in James 1:9).

This is not to say that God loves the rich less than he loves the poor, or that the poor somehow deserve the sacrificial death of Jesus less than the rich. But it is to say that God is choosing to bless the very people James's readers (then and now) tend to shun.

A Gospel Trend, Not a Statistical One

James' point is more than one of incidental observation. This is about more than statistical trends; it reflects something of the very gospel itself. Jesus himself said that it was hard for a rich man to enter the kingdom of God (Mark 10:24-25). The message of the gospel to anyone is deeply humbling, for it makes it abundantly clear that we cannot save ourselves. No one is able to make themselves right with God by their own ingenuity or legwork. Jesus did not come to offer himself as a top-up to what we have already managed to achieve, to make up the difference between our existing spiritual capital and what God actually demands. The claim of Jesus is that we need him to do it all for us—every last bit. We have nothing at all to contribute.

It is therefore fitting that God should be choosing many from among the poor. Their very lowly economic status is a visual aid of where all people are before God. It is fitting that nobodies are coming to Christ, for Christ himself became the ultimate Nobody for our sake. His cross is itself a symbol of weakness and poverty: "For you know the grace of our Lord Jesus Christ, that though he was rich, yet for your sake he became poor, so that you through his poverty might become rich" (2 Corinthians 8:9). It seems appropriate that those through whom the message of that cross is to be spread are predominantly poor.

James' words are a warning that we are not to think that reaching the rich and powerful with the gospel is more strategic than reaching the poor. It is easy for Christians to find themselves thinking that if only we could get a sports star, or celebrity, or high-profile leader converted, then it would be a great coup for the gospel. Such people, by virtue of their position, are deemed to be more strategically valuable than others, and so resources are apportioned accordingly. They are reckoned to be the key to reaching society as a whole. And so if a professional footballer comes into church at the same time as a tramp, it's the footballer that becomes the focus of attention.

> We are not to think that reaching the rich and powerful with the gospel is more strategic than reaching the poor.

For a number of years I worked for a church in central Oxford and oversaw the **ministry** to students at the university. I lost count of the number of times people would say to me: "It's great that you're doing that work. Oxford students are so strategically important." It was something that made me feel deeply uncomfortable. It assumed that, because of who they are in the world, Oxford students are more significant for the spread of the kingdom. But the only reason that ministry to Oxford students matters is the same reason that ministry to anyone matters: they are lost souls that Jesus came to seek and save.

It is not because their academic abilities make them more strategically useful. In fact, the last thing many such students need to be told is that they are strategically important!

The same principle applies to any ministry focused on the wealthy and privileged in society. There are many fine examples of these kinds of ministries. But it is important that those involved in such work check that they're involved for the right reasons. The privileged need reaching because they are lost, not because they matter more than anyone else. Building a gospel strategy around "key people" in society contradicts the very insight that James is drawing to our attention. God's strategy, by and large, is to use the weak things of the world to achieve his purposes.

This should not surprise us. We follow a crucified criminal. He had nowhere to lay his head (Luke 9:58). "There were many who were appalled at him—his appearance was so disfigured beyond that of any human being" (Isaiah 52:14). This was the man who for all our sakes became poor and embraced poverty (2 Corinthians 8:9). Would we rush to welcome him into our church? Would we have thought him "strategically important"? Would he look like someone worth watching for future Christian leadership?

There is a further irony to the favouritism of James' readers. It is the rich, of all people, who are giving his Christian readers a hard time.

"Is it not the rich who are exploiting you? Are they not the ones who are dragging you into court? Are they not the ones who are blaspheming the noble name of him to whom you belong?" (James **2:6b-7**)

The rich are causing trouble for the church: exploiting them, cleaning them out in the courts, and speaking foulness of Jesus Christ.

James is not saying this to engender resentment towards the rich, but to point out the irony of Christians pinning their hopes on them. Christians exalting the rich and powerful go right against the grain of how God is at work, and of the gospel itself. God's ways are not the world's ways. Neither should ours be.

Questions for reflection

1. Have you ever been subjected to favouritism by someone else? How did it make you feel?

2. How does the truth of James 2:5 both encourage and humble you?

3. Are you in danger of showing favouritism in some way? How? How will you use the gospel to change your heart?

PART TWO

James has already provided one compelling reason why Christians should not show favouritism. It goes against what we have seen of God's work in choosing the poor to be rich in faith (**v 5**). That in itself is reason enough, but James follows it with two more reasons. Favouritism contradicts not only God's choice, but also God's law and God's mercy.

Favouritism and God's Law

James draws his readers' attention to Old Testament law. To love our neighbours as ourselves means we are keeping "the royal law found in Scripture"—we "are doing right" (**v 8**). "But if you show favouritism, you sin and are convicted by the law as law-breakers" (**v 9**).

Favouritism breaks the law. This bears repeating: when we show favouritism, we break God's perfect law. James in particular highlights the command given to the Israelites to love their neighbours as themselves (see Leviticus 19:18). James's selection of this particular command is not random. It is the Old Testament verse Jesus quoted the most. It may not be going too far to claim it was his favourite Old Testament commandment. It was this passage (along with Deuteronomy 6:4-5) that Jesus pointed to when asked to provide an **executive summary** of the whole of God's law (Mark 12:28-31). Loving our neighbours as ourselves sums up everything God wants from the behaviour of his people towards others. It is **biblical ethics** in a nutshell—God's law in a bullet-point. As well as being Jesus' way of summarising the law of God, this command was the basis for one of his most famous parables. The Parable of the Good Samaritan (Luke 10:25-37) was told specifically to explain something of what it means to keep this commandment.

It is because Jesus put this command front and centre that James can call it the "royal law" in James **2:8**; the King himself repeatedly emphasised it.

James mentions it now because it may have been a way in which his readers were justifying favouritism. We can imagine them thinking to themselves how well they are doing at keeping the law at this point—it tells them to love their neighbours, and that is precisely what they believe themselves to be doing. But they only love *some* of their neighbours—the rich and powerful. And to keep the law only selectively is actually to break it. The law is of a piece. It all hangs together. It is integrated. To break one part is to break the whole thing: "Whoever keeps the whole law and yet stumbles at just one point is guilty of breaking all of it" (**v 10**).

> The law hangs together. To break one part is to break the whole thing.

Once, when I was a kid, and with considerable help from my older brother (he was supposed to be in goal), I managed to break the large window in the French doors that led from the lounge into the garden. The moment it happened, I knew I was going to be in trouble. I also wondered why it had never occurred to me that kicking a heavy ball around indoors near large windows might end this way, especially given my brother's goalkeeping skills. When, moments later, my parents were alerted to the wreckage taking place under their roof, they were not best pleased, and all future indoor football games were immediately postponed indefinitely.

Imagine how this would have played as a defence: *Look, the ball only hit one part of the window. And look at how much of the window isn't broken...* The fact was that the window was broken. It didn't matter where it was broken, or in how many places the impact was made; what was significant was that it *was* broken.

It is the same with God's law. Fawning and fussing over selected high-powered and wealthy neighbours—or loving our neighbours when they are impressive, or similar to us—does not cover the fact that others are being quietly but studiously ignored. Selective obedience to a command is actually disobedience to the whole thing.

So too is only obeying some commands while overlooking other ones. The One who rules out adultery also outlaws murder. If I avoid one but commit the other, I "have become a law-breaker" (**v 11**).

I have only been on jury duty once, and so have not seen the inside of a courtroom much. Frankly, I was disappointed by the lack of grandstanding and fisticuffs that movies had taught me were part of every trial. But imagine that we are members of the jury, and that someone is on trial for murder. The evidence is overwhelming: DNA, closed-circuit TV footage, multiple credible witnesses. There can be no mistaking that the suspect is guilty; he practically admits as much under cross-examination. But before the inevitable verdict is announced, the defendant announces that he wants to make one more statement in his own defence. Before a hushed court, and with utter self-belief, he proceeds to tell the jury what an impeccable and faithful husband he has been. Yes, he has killed a man—he has murdered someone. But he has never committed adultery. Not once, not ever.

We do not need to be Perry Mason (the fictional criminal-defence lawyer) to see the flaw in the logic. Good behaviour in one area does not cancel out law-breaking in another. It doesn't work before a judge and jury, and nor does it work before God. Yet how often we try it! *No,* says James. *Once a law is broken, the law is broken.*

The reason for this is clear: the same Lawgiver stands behind all of the commandments. The same God who prohibits adultery also prohibits murder. There is one mind behind the whole of the law and all its constituent parts. There is a unity to it, because God himself is one (as Jesus reminded his listeners when he gave his summary of the law). We cannot think we can pick and choose which bits we honour.

Failing to love our neighbours in the way God requires is to break God's law. It is to break the very law that Jesus says sums up the whole of God's will for our behaviour towards others. Readers of James' letter who are pulling out all the stops for the rich and powerful must not think how well they are doing: *Wow, I'm really loving my neighbour!* They have no reason to congratulate themselves while other, more needy people around them are being neglected. God's law condemns such favouritism.

Favouritism and God's Mercy

James now begins to conclude his argument against favouritism: "Speak and act as those who are going to be judged by the law that gives freedom" (**v 12**).

We have already seen how the perfect law gives freedom (1:25). Living God's ways will always be best for us. We are to speak and act in the light of all that Jesus calls us to do.

But now James adds that this law will judge us in some way. It will expose the kinds of lives we have led, and whether or not we have been impacted and shaped by a real faith in Christ.

Obedience to Christ's ways is the sign that we have been saved by him—that his death and resurrection have truly gripped us. As James is about to demonstrate next in chapter 2, true faith changes us. It can be and will be seen in how we live. The transformation will not be all at once, and may in fact be gradual. But it will be unmistakable. The evidence that we have real, authentic saving faith is that we put it into practice. As we have seen, James has already told us something of what this will look like:

"Religion that God our Father accepts as pure and faultless is this: to look after orphans and widows in their distress and to keep oneself from being polluted by the world." (1:27)

Part of the visible outworking of true Christianity is compassion for the needy: to be moved by the distress of the most destitute, and provoked into taking action to help them. Another way of putting this is to say that true Christianity is seen in how believers show mercy to others around them.

This is not arbitrary. The fact that showing mercy to others is a sign of being a true follower of Christ is not surprising, because the very heart of what Christ has come to do is showing mercy.

We demonstrate that we have received mercy from Christ when we show it to others. Mercy defines the gospel: Christ loved us even when we were unlovely in his sight; he gave promises to us that we did not deserve; and he showered us with blessings we could never have earned. Having been treated in this way, we will instinctively start to treat others in the same way. There is no other way to make a human being merciful than for them to become gripped and defined by the mercy of God to them. Jesus said: "Blessed are the merciful, for they will be shown mercy" (Matthew 5:7). James puts it the other way round: "Judgment without mercy will be shown to anyone who has not been merciful" (James **2:13**).

> We demonstrate we have received mercy from Christ when we show it to others. Mercy defines the gospel.

Those who do not show mercy will not receive it. Why? Because their very lack of mercy shows they have never properly received the gospel. The proof that someone has been captivated by God's mercy in Christ is that they display it to others. Blomberg and Kamell write:

"Those who never show any mercy cannot have internalized and accepted God's mercy." (Blomberg and Kamell, page 120).

In fact, this is the point James has been making all along. He began this section on favouritism by saying: "My brothers and sisters, believers in our glorious Lord Jesus Christ must not show favouritism" (**v 1**). Christians are "believers in our glorious Lord Jesus Christ". Literally, we are believers "in our Lord Jesus Christ of the glory". What is that "glory"? It is his death, resurrection and exaltation. As he prayed to the Father on the eve of his crucifixion, Jesus said: "Father, the hour has come. Glorify your Son, that your Son may glorify you … I have brought you glory on earth by finishing the work you gave me to do" (John 17:1, 4). Jesus was glorified as he died on the cross, for that is where he most brought glory to the Father. It is through the cross that God is glorified. The cross demonstrates his love (Romans 5:8), his wisdom (1 Corinthians 1:23-24), and his justice (Romans 3:25-26). It is here that the light of God's revelation reaches its fullest midday height.

And yet the death of Jesus brought God glory through foolishness (1 Corinthians 1:23), servitude (Philippians 2:7), and deprivation (2 Corinthians 8:9). It is in *these* things that we see God reconciling us to himself. Jesus allowed himself to hang in humiliation, nakedness and shame. This is the cross in which we boast. Jesus embraced poverty so that, in him and through him, we might become rich.

Understanding this utterly redefines what we consider to be glorious. When the cross of Christ becomes the benchmark, the world's glory looks very unimpressive indeed. If it is the glory of Jesus—or rather, the Jesus "of the glory"—that we most long for, we will not be impressed or captivated by the riches and glories of the world around us. As James has already shown us, such things are as fleeting and momentary as the beauty of wild flowers in the desert (James 1:10). Instead, it will be the mercy that God has poured over us through the lowliness of Christ that will most attract our hearts.

It is only once this has happened that we will be those characterised by mercy towards the lowly rather than favouritism towards the rich. When we find ourselves tending towards the latter and neglecting the former, the solution is not more effort or gritting our teeth and getting on with it. What changes us is looking again at the glory of Jesus. At the cross we see the true dimensions of God's love and mercy, and the full mega-wattage of his glory. It is as we gaze on this (and only as we gaze on this) that we become naturally merciful ourselves.

Questions for reflection

1. How has this passage changed your view of and feelings about God's law?

2. Are you in any way using obeying the law in one way as an excuse for ignoring God's commands in a different area of life?

3. Reflect on God's mercy to you in Christ. Is there anyone to whom you need to extend that same quality of mercy, today?

5. FAITH WORKS

A politician waxes lyrical about the high standards of the local state schools in his area, but enrols his own children in an expensive private college. A McDonald's executive claims his company offers the best family food, but is found taking his family out for a meal at Burger King. A husband insists he cherishes his wife and yet maintains a secret, longstanding affair with another woman.

In each of these examples there is a difference between what is claimed and what is done. The actions do not match the words. It is the behaviour of these people that shows what they really think, more than what they say. Our claims are not always an accurate reflection of what we really think and believe—but our deeds are. We do not always live what we say we believe—but we do always believe what we live out.

This is no less true for Christians, and this is James' concern in this passage. In what will become something of a trademark in this letter, James begins with some arresting questions: "What good is it, my brothers and sisters, if someone claims to have faith but has no deeds? Can such faith save them?" (**2:14**).

It is easy to claim to have faith. It does not take much to say you are a Christian. National surveys in Western countries continue to reflect high numbers of people who do this very thing. It is as easy as saying a few words, checking a box on a form, making a comment on Facebook, or answering a question in a survey. Faith is easily claimed, but James says it may not be genuine Christian faith.

The stakes could not be higher. In the questions posed above, James assumes a negative answer. It is no good to claim faith without any kind of deeds to give that claim credibility. However easy it might be to profess to be a Christian, and whatever someone might feel that profession achieves for them, James says it accomplishes absolutely nothing good at all if mere profession is all it is. It is useless. In fact, it is worse than useless. Hence the answer to his second question. Such "faith" cannot save.

Here is the genuinely frightening truth that should give you and me pause. It is possible to claim, *and to believe you possess*, genuine saving faith when in fact you do not. It is possible, in other words, to believe you have things sorted with God—that you will not face his judgment, that there is hope for you beyond the grave—and yet remain under the judgment of God. It is possible, in short, unknowingly to possess counterfeit faith.

It is natural for James to raise this at this point in his letter. He has already shown us the deeds that true Christian faith should lead to (1:27), and has provided an example of how some of his readers are failing to demonstrate some of those deeds through showing favouritism to the rich. Claiming faith but lacking deeds seems to be a pertinent issue.

How can we tell if we possess true faith? is the most important question we can ask, and the most crucial to answer accurately.

So how can we tell if we possess true faith? What are the marks of saving faith? How can we know if we possess it—if we really are "believers in our glorious Lord Jesus Christ" (2:1)? For anyone who professes to be a Christian, this is the most important question we can ask, and the most crucial to answer accurately.

James answers the question both negatively and positively here. First, he shows what is lacking in counterfeit faith; then, what the signs of genuine faith are. For each, he provides two examples.

Counterfeit Faith

In the first example of **spurious** faith, James imagines a Christian who "is without clothes and daily food" (**v 15**). What do you do? Do you say: "Go in peace; keep warm and well fed" (**v 16**)? If you do, but do "nothing about their physical needs, what good is it?" James repeats his point: "In the same way, faith by itself, if it is not accompanied by action, is dead" (**v 17**).

James' example is hypothetical, but entirely conceivable. We know there were destitute believers among the churches he was writing to. He has already spoken of those "in humble circumstances" (1:9), and of Christians being exploited and taken to court by the rich (2:6). It is not hard to imagine some of these Christians finding themselves in the situation James imagines.

Sadly, too, the response in this scenario is also conceivable. Merely wishing someone well in the face of both their need and our ability to help is an indication that our spoken sentiments are not sincere. If we have the means to help meet the practical need before us, and choose not to, no amount of nice-sounding words will make up for it. Twice, James asks, "What good is it?" (**v 14, 16**). Words without corresponding deeds are just empty sounds. Useless. They mean nothing. Our words sound fine, while our lack of actions shout: *I don't really mean this.*

But James' use of this scenario is not merely illustrative—an example of a words-and-actions mismatch. The very scenario itself—a believer in serious material need—is one that Christians are to care deeply about.

James' expectation is that genuine believers will do all they can to help one another practically. In the example he has given, it is a fellow Christian who is in need ("a brother or a sister", **v 15**). Our obligations to help the needy extend beyond our local church fellowship of course. Jesus's parable of the Good Samaritan (Luke 10:25-37) is a call to be a good neighbour to all, irrespective of how unconnected we might be to them. But within a general obligation to help the needy, we have a particular responsibility to those within our Christian communities. So Paul can say: "Let us do good to all people, especially to those who belong to the family of believers" (Galatians 6:10).

Being presented with such a need, possessing the means to help meet that need, and yet not doing so is, once again, worse than useless. It is a sign of a lifeless, false faith. Deedless Christianity is dead Christianity. It is counterfeit. Faith that has no impact on behaviour is not authentic Christian faith. Real faith acts. Real love does. And in particular, real faith serves and cares for others, especially fellow believers.

What Jesus Saw

James' next case study makes the point even more forcefully. Now he imagines an objector, who says: "You have faith; I have deeds" (James **2:18**). In other words: *James, there are different types of Christian out there. We don't all have the same strong point. We have our own way of being a Christian. Some are the thinky types, forever reading up on their doctrine and getting everything pinned down. Then there are us practical types; we're into doing rather than reflecting. You've got your faith, and I've got my deeds. You say potato; I say potahto.*

But this kind of distinction doesn't wash with James. His response is: "Show me your faith without deeds, and I will show you my faith by my deeds" (**v 18**). There aren't it's-all-in-my-head Christians and my-faith-is-what-I-do Christians. There is genuine faith and there is spurious faith; and genuine, saving, get-you-to-heaven faith will always be expressed in how we live. There is no other way to demonstrate it. Faith is seen in deeds. No amount of chin-stroking or verbal footwork will get round that. True faith is seen in action. There is no other way to see it. Faith is shown by deeds.

We have an illustration of this from the life of Jesus. There was a famous occasion when Jesus was teaching a crowd jam-packed into a small home in Capernaum (Mark 2:1-12). There wasn't even room outside. The place was overflowing. And so when a group of men turned up, desperate to get to Jesus, the only option was to climb up onto the flat roof and start burrowing through into the room below. No doubt things quickly ground to a halt as dust and stones began to fall, and bright sunlight and then faces appeared above. The reason for this desperate entry is clear: they wanted to bring a paralysed man to Jesus.

Once they had lowered this man onto the floor in front of Jesus, Mark tells us something that is much missed, but greatly significant: "When Jesus saw their faith, he said to the paralysed man, 'Son, your sins are forgiven'" (v 5). What did Jesus see? Their faith. Their faith was a physically visible thing. All true faith is. It is not an invisible way of thinking about God; it is something seen in how people behave. True faith can be seen; counterfeit faith is invisible.

Even the Demons...

If that was not enough, James drives the point home even more sharply: "You believe that there is one God. Good! Even the demons believe that" (James **2:19**)

Now the gloves are off. There is no area of Christian belief more significant than this. God is One. It is the cornerstone of a biblical understanding of God: "Hear, O Israel: the LORD our God, the LORD is one" (Deuteronomy 6:4). So significant was this verse that committed Old Testament believers would recite it every single day. Foundational to everything else they knew about God was that he is One.

Jesus himself also affirmed the importance of this, quoting this very verse when asked to give his executive summary of the law (Mark 12:29). It is a truth that has been given pride of place in the great creeds of the Christian church: "We believe in one God". It is an affirmation made by countless Christians every single week as they gather together and declare what they believe.

And yet... affirmation of Christian truth—however central and orthodox that truth may be—is not enough. It means nothing. To any who are tempted to reduce genuine Christianity to saying the right things, James points to an uncomfortable yet undeniable truth: "The demons believe that" (James **2:19**).

If we are ever tempted to congratulate ourselves about our ortho-doxy—about having our theology right—we need to remember who we share it with. The demons have sound doctrine. This should not surprise us. They came from heaven, after all. They know who God is. They know he is One. There are no atheists in the demonic realm. Affirming certain right things about God is clearly not enough. Hell is full of good theology. Pleased with your right understanding of who God is? Congratulations: you are at precisely the same level as the demons.

> The demons have sound doctrine—hell is full of good theology.

Not only that: James also points out that these demons "shudder" (**v 19**). They're not unaffected by what they know about God—they know enough of God's greatness to tremble at him. Of course, true Christians will rejoice at the thought of our great God and Father, rather than shuddering and cowering. But James is likely highlighting how the de-mons are impacted by what they know to be true. How do you know they believe there is one God? They shudder. You can see their belief.

Who God is should not be taken lightly. It is all too easy to trot out a line of the creed without really thinking about it or meaning it. There being one God is a weighty matter. The demons know that who God is matters. Do we?

Profession of belief without deeds is no more than hot air. It is the mark of counterfeit faith—all claim, all about saying the right thing; and no actual difference to how we live. Such a faith cannot save (**v 14**). Such a faith is dead (**v 17**). Someone saying they believe some-thing is no real indication of whether they really do. It is their actions that show if it is real.

This is why we need to treat national surveys of belief with caution. It is common in many western countries for a huge proportion of the populous to claim that they believe in God, and even in Jesus Christ. It can be tempting for Christians to regard this as a "win" for our side. But according to James, such results prove very little. A national survey or census merely records what people say they believe. To find out what they do believe, we would need to see them in action.

James' concern here is that we look at ourselves, not at the nominalism we might happen to see around us. His words are (as ever) very searching. We can be so quick to affirm our faith—to declare it in creeds and songs, prayers and conversations—that we never stop to examine whether our profession of faith is truly credible. Immediately I hear myself thinking: *Of course I'm a Christian—I've always said I am,* I need to stop and examine what is going on in my life. I need to look at my own heart. Loving saying that I'm a Christian is not the proof that I am one. I am in as much danger as anyone of possessing counterfeit faith, and I am a fool if I think otherwise.

Real faith is not merely sentimental (wishing someone well while doing nothing to help them), and it is not merely credal (affirming something to be true but which makes no difference to the way we live). Such things may be something, but they are not Christianity. And they do not save.

Questions for reflection

1. What evidence is there that your faith is not merely "sentimental"?

2. What evidence is there that your faith is not merely "credal"?

3. How do these verses move you to pray to "our glorious Lord Jesus Christ" (2:1)?

PART TWO

The Patriarch

James has shown us counterfeit faith and provided two examples: the armchair **philanthropist**, and the doctrinally orthodox demon. Both illustrate how claims that are not corroborated by deeds are worthless. Now he turns to the nature of genuine faith and once again provides a couple of worked examples, this time from the Old Testament—Abraham and Rahab.

James starts with Abraham, and with good reason. Abraham was not just a man of faith; he was the **archetypal** man of faith. He is "God's friend" (**v 23**) and "our father" (**v 21**). If you can prove a point from Abraham, you've won the argument! This is the trump card.

So, we're asked: "Do you want evidence that faith without deeds is useless?" (**v 20**). There's a sense in which we shouldn't need these verses, unless we're "foolish". By now we should have got the point. James has just proved his case using the example of demons. We passed the **QED** point quite some time ago. Only a fool would need any further persuasion—but James isn't going to make any assumptions about us! We don't just need to get this; we really, really need to get it. So, to Abraham:

> "Was not our father Abraham considered righteous for what he did when he offered his son Isaac on the altar? You see that his faith and his actions were working together, and his faith was made complete by what he did. And the scripture was fulfilled that says, 'Abraham believed God, and it was credited to him as righteousness,' and he was called God's friend." (**v 21-23**)

James takes us back to some key events in Abraham's life and shows us how they are connected. In Genesis 22 Abraham was told to sacrifice his son Isaac, then only a boy. Humanly speaking it made little sense. Quite apart from the question mark over sacrificing your own child was the additional fact that it seemed to contradict everything

God had said he was going to do for Abraham. Counter-intuitive doesn't begin to describe it.

Earlier in Genesis 12, God had first called Abraham and had given him a set of promises, not least of which was that he would be the father of a great nation (Genesis 12:1-3). Everything hinged on having a line of descendants. But at that stage Abraham was old and his wife was barren, and so having just one child, let alone a dynasty, was going to be a challenge. So God restated the promise, adding that Abraham's descendants would be as numerous as the stars in the sky (Genesis 15:5). Abraham believed God. And, James reminds us, this "was credited to him as righteousness" (James **2:23**; Genesis 15:6). He was right with God. And in due course Isaac was born.

Yet, in Genesis 22, we see Abraham prepared to sacrifice Isaac in obedience to God—he "offered his son Isaac on the altar" (James **2:21**). In the end he didn't need to; God provided an animal as a substitute. But the point is that Abraham was willing to obey. And this is why it's significant: it proves he really did trust God. The obedience of Abraham (seen in Genesis 22) demonstrated the genuineness of his faith (seen in Genesis 15). "His faith and his actions were working together"—his actions "complete" his faith (James **2:22**). His faith was seen in his obedience. The kind of faith that had been credited to Abraham as righteousness years before in Genesis 15 now produced this act of obedience in Genesis 22—the kind of act only a man of faith would perform, the kind of act that causes the doer to be "considered righteous" (James **2:21**).

This leads James to the first of two conclusions, and initially it looks troubling: "You see that a person is considered righteous by what they do and not by faith alone" (**v 24**). On the surface, James seems to be flatly contradicting the apostle Paul. Consider the following statements from Paul:

"For we maintain that a person is justified by faith apart from the works of the law." (Romans 3:28)

"For it is by grace you have been saved, through faith—and this is not from yourselves, it is the gift of God—not by works, so that no one can boast." (Ephesians 2:8-9)

Paul is emphatic. We are justified by faith alone, and not by our works.

But James is equally emphatic. We are justified by what we do, and not by faith alone. The two New Testament writers seem diametrically opposed and, if that wasn't problematic enough, the issue over which they seem opposed could not be more important. It's not as if they're disagreeing over the colour of Moses' hair, or what Jesus's great-aunt was called. This is about how we are justified—how we are put right with God. Disagreeing over this is disagreeing over what Christianity is really about. It could not be more serious.

> The obedience of Abraham demonstrated the genuineness of his faith.

It is no surprise that this passage from James has often been used as evidence that the Bible is contradictory, that it has no unity, and cannot easily be trusted as the reliable word of God. Little wonder that great Christians from the past, like Martin Luther, have balked somewhat at James! The presence of a verse like this in the Bible looks as if it could unravel everything.

But before we join in with such conclusions, there are important observations to make about this purported contradiction. The first thing to note is that James would not have been unfamiliar with the teachings of Paul. The two had met and knew each other. It is highly unlikely that James wouldn't have come across Paul's formulation of salvation being "by faith alone". Before we write James off as having a contradictory understanding of salvation, or write this verse off as James having a colossal "oopsy", we need to allow for the possibility that James might in fact be offering a corrective not to Paul himself, but to *followers* of Paul who have taken his "faith alone" teaching in unwise directions.

Paul's writings themselves show awareness that some believers had indeed been doing this. In his letter to the Romans, he alludes to ways in which people had been misunderstanding his teaching on justification:

"Why not say—as some slanderously claim that we say—'Let us do evil that good may result'?" (Romans 3:8)

People were taking Paul's words and distorting their meaning. His teaching was being used to promote a glib attitude to sin and repentance, which took being justified by faith alone to mean that people could come to Christ for forgiveness and then sin with impunity. There is every possibility that James is targeting such misappropriation of Paul's teaching, rather than the teaching itself. Both Paul and James, after all, are agreed on the necessity of love flowing from true faith. Paul frequently drew his readers' attention to the necessity of love. Most famously, he reminded the church in Corinth that without love even the most radical gifting and sacrifice come to naught (1 Corinthians 13:1-3). Professed faith without love counts for nothing.

Next, we need to notice that James has been using the word "faith" in a slightly different way from Paul. For Paul, faith is trusting Christ; we are saved by faith alone, because it is the saving work of Christ alone that we trust. But James has been using "faith" more broadly, describing not just trust in Christ, but the *claim* to be trusting in Christ. Hence his question at the start of this section about the person who professes faith but has no deeds: "Can such *faith* save them?" (James **2:14**, my emphasis). Faith here refers to their profession of trust.

Finally, closer inspection of what James is actually saying helps us to see that his aim is quite specific. He is not making a sweeping generalisation about how we are saved, still less one which is at odds with his apostolic colleague, Paul. Look again at what James is saying in the first part of this key verse:

"You *see* that a person is considered righteous by what they do and not by faith alone." (**v 24**, my emphasis)

We easily skim over those first couple of words, but they are crucial for understanding what James is (and isn't) saying. We might easily use the words "You see" in a somewhat innocuous way, to introduce the thought we're about to expound. In this sense it is equivalent to "You know", or "Now then". You see, that's how we often mean it.

But we can also use it literally: you see that I spilled ketchup down my shirt this morning. It is a thing visually apparent to anyone near enough to notice. James seems to be using the words in this sense. "You see that a person is considered righteous..." means James is talking not about how someone is justified, but how you see—how you can tell—that someone is truly justified. His concern is not with the means of justification, but with the visible evidence for it. This, after all, is the exact point James has been making throughout this passage.

We're now in a position to see what James is doing in this verse. How can you tell if someone is justified? How do you know if they're considered righteous by God? The answer is not by mere profession of faith. Anyone can claim to be trusting in Christ. You could train a parrot to say it. No, "faith alone" (in the sense James is using it in these verses) is insufficient. The real evidence is how that faith moves someone to obey what God has said to them—what Paul called "the obedience that comes from faith" (Romans 1:5). As Christians have often summarised it, Paul shows us we are saved by faith alone; James shows us that saving faith never remains alone. It is seen in godly deeds. Just look at Abraham.

The Prostitute

And look also, says James, at Rahab (James **2:25**).

Rahab could hardly be more different from Abraham. He was a Jewish man; she was a Gentile woman. He was rich; she was poor. He was a patriarch; she was a prostitute. Yet they both illustrate the same point: true faith is shown by actions, and this choice of example shows us that it comes in all shapes and sizes.

We come across Rahab early in the book of Joshua. The people of

God are poised to enter the **promised land** and will need to take the city of Jericho. Spies are dispatched to case the joint before battle is joined. During their reconnaissance they come across Rahab. Word has got out that Jewish spies are in the city, and the Jericho police are knocking at the door; yet Rahab covers for them, sending the police off in the wrong direction and slipping the spies out (Joshua 2:1-21). These actions align her with the mission of the Israelites, but put her entirely at cross-purposes with her own people. It is incredibly risky. Yet she does it all because she has faith in God. She says to the spies:

"I know that the LORD has given this land to you and that a great fear of you has fallen on us, so that all who live in this country are melting in fear because of you. We have heard how the LORD dried up the water of the Red Sea for you when you came out of Egypt, and what you did to Sihon and Og, the two kings of the Amorites east of the Jordan, whom you completely destroyed. When we heard of it, our hearts sank and everyone's courage failed because of you, for the LORD your God is God in heaven above and on the earth below." (v 9-11)

Along with many others, Rahab has heard of God and of what he has done in fulfilling his promises to his people. She knows him to be the Lord over all. And because she believes all this, she acts. She doesn't just offer a parting *I hope it all works out for you guys*; she lives her life in the light of the reality she now understands to be true. She demonstrates and proves her faith by what she does.

So James comes to his conclusion: "As the body without the spirit is dead, so faith without deeds is dead" (James **2:26**). I have seen a dead body on a handful of occasions. As a pastor, I am not entirely unfamiliar with the workings of undertakers. In each case, they had done a good job in making the body look as presentable as possible—to make it look as much as possible as though the deceased was merely resting their eyes. But for all surface appearances, there is no mistaking a dead body. It is motionless, cold, and the fingernails are already changing colour.

It is this image of lifelessness that James uses to hammer home his point. Professions of faith—claims to be trusting in Christ and believing in God—can look superficially impressive, and even move us. But without deeds, they are no more vibrant than a dead body awaiting the grave. In another context, we might have expected this verse to be the other way around: without faith, deeds are dead. That is true. But that is not the point James needs to make and that his readers need to understand. Unless it is lived out, faith is no more useful than a breathless corpse—and no amount of careful presentation can change that.

Real faith is lived-out faith. True faith is visible and active. It does things. We do not always live what we say we believe or even think we believe, but we do always believe what we live out. So the question is: are we demonstrating deeds that come from true faith? Or are we in danger of hiding behind claims of faith that have no evidence from our lifestyle?

The Patriarch, the Prostitute, and You

This passage requires self-examination from all of us. We need to reflect on what we are doing, and how (or if) that relates to what we say and think about ourselves. As I write this I am conscious that we respond to challenges like this in quite different ways. Some of us will naturally have very tender consciences: any time a challenge like this comes along, we instantly think of our inconsistencies and faults. They are never too far from our minds. And so we might easily find ourselves questioning whether we really are Christians at all. (And if we are the kind of person I am describing, it might be that we often question this.)

It is a blessing to have a tender conscience—but the danger is that we so consider our deficiencies that we fail to notice the ways in which we do actually (if imperfectly) express our faith in our actions. We only see the flaws and we easily miss what might be genuine fruit.

Others of us may have the opposite reaction. We immediately assume we're fine. We run a cursory self-diagnostic, think of a handful
of good Christian deeds we've done recently, check the "James 2"
box, and then move on. But just as the tender conscience might overlook genuine good, so too the naturally
confident might overlook some genuine problems. We see the good deeds
and miss the many sinful attitudes bub-
bling away under the surface.

> Real faith is
> lived-out faith.
> It does things.

In both cases, our self-assessment is
superficial. We need to take our time,
and we need God's help. We need to pray with David: "But who can
discern their own errors? Forgive my hidden faults" (Psalm 19:12). We
need God to show us where we are truly at, especially if we know we
are prone to have a very slanted view of ourselves. One of the means
God can use, of course, is Christian people who know us well and
who will be honest with us—and we then need to be willing to hear
their answer, whether it confirms or corrects what we think.

There may be some who read this part of James and rightly conclude that they are not Christians. That is part of James' aim after all—
to expose false faith. Though that might sound like a negative aim to
have, it is enormously important. As we've seen, such (counterfeit)
faith does us no good at all. To realise that is an essential and positive
step. We need to jettison false faith if we are to enjoy true faith. The
best way to respond in such situations is to pray to God about it: to
confess the false faith and ask him for true faith. In fact, asking for
faith is itself one of the first signs that God is giving it to us!

Questions for reflection

1. Imagine someone suggested to you that James and Paul contradict each other. How would you, in a minute, explain what both say about faith, and how both are in agreement?

2. Do you, by character, tend to have a tender conscience, or a complacent one? How has that influenced your reaction to this passage?

3. Do you need to speak to someone else about your own faith? When will you do this? Are you ready to listen?

6. WORSE THAN STICKS AND STONES

"Sticks and stones may break my bones, but words will never hurt me."

This is the ditty that many of us will have heard as children, and which many of us may now be passing on as parents. It is memorable—but it is inaccurate. We live in a world where words matter. They have the capacity to affect us enormously. The damage done by something said can go far deeper and last much longer than damage done by sticks and stones.

This should not surprise us. Our God, after all, is a speaking God. And his speaking is not an incidental part of his nature. It is central. He created the very universe we live in by speaking (Genesis 1:3; Hebrews 11:3). He continues to relate to us and to work in us by his words.

But when it comes to our words and their impact, it is a very different story. The US President Abraham Lincoln reputedly said: "I would rather remain silent and be thought a fool, than speak up and remove all doubt." While we understand the point he is making (even if we often forget to apply it to ourselves!), we nevertheless need to recognise that there is a far greater danger than being regarded by others as a fool. For reasons more important than looking foolish, we need to come to terms with our tongues and what we say. James has already flagged this issue up for us: "Those who consider themselves religious and yet do not keep a tight rein on their tongues deceive themselves, and their religion is worthless" (1:26). One of the marks of authentic Christian behaviour is control of our speech.

James begins chapter 3 with a warning for would-be pastors: "Not many of you should become teachers, my fellow believers, because you know that we who teach will be judged more strictly" (**3:1**). He is talking about teaching in the church, and warns that we shouldn't rush into this kind of role. Teachers will be judged more strictly because they have the capacity to do particular damage to the church. Their words will either convey the truth, or obscure and even deny it. We need to pray for those in our churches who teach.

> Bible teachers' words will either convey the truth, or obscure or even deny it.

James highlights something that is a particular issue for teachers in the church, but which is a general issue for all believers—the importance of keeping the tongue in check. The situation described in **verse 2** is not as hypothetical as some translations make it look. James is not describing someone who is never at fault, but someone who generally doesn't stumble in what they say. Such a person is not perfect in the sense of being sinless, but they are complete and mature. (The word used is the same in 1:4, where it describes the person who has been made complete through perseverance.) In other words, James is reiterating the point he made in 1:26: a mark of authentic Christian faith is keeping a tight rein on our tongues. Someone who can control their tongue in check can "keep their whole body in check" (**3:2**).

To control your tongue, you need to understand it, and so—like a doctor—James is asking us to open our mouths, and stick out our tongues so that he can give us a good examination. There are a number of things we need to see.

Powerful

To show us how powerful our tongues are, James provides us with two visual aids—horses (**v 3**) and ships (**v 4**). I'm not great with horses. I've been riding a few times, and each time it has been terrifying. It is only when I'm sitting on one that I realise just how big they are. I'm intimidated and they're incompliant, which is not a great combination. I'll just have to take James' word for it that they can actually be controlled. But the key is what actually does the controlling: a small piece of metal called a bit, which sits in the horse's mouth and can be used by its rider to direct it. That whole animal can be controlled and manipulated by something so small.

We see the same idea with ships. Ships are big. Rudders are small. One of the biggest ships in the world is the US aircraft carrier, *USS Eisenhower.* It weighs over 91,000 tons, is nearly 1,100 feet in length, has a nuclear–powered 280,000-horsepower engine, a complement of 6,100 men and women, and carries nearly 100 aircraft. It is vast. It is like a floating city. And yet all that weight, personnel, and hardware are steered by a rudder that's just a tenth of one percent of the ship's size. Something so comparatively small is able to manoeuvre something so huge.

James says it is the same with the tongue. It is small but very, very powerful, and so it can make "great boasts" (**v 5**). I'm told it is less than half a percent of our body weight. (I've not found a pain-free way to verify that, so we'll have to assume it's true.) Yet despite its small size, the tongue has an enormous impact. Its effect on us is out of all proportion to its size. It is able to determine the very course of our lives. The chances are you can think of things you have said, or not said, that have changed the path of your life, for better or for worse.

So far, so potentially good, we might think. The tongue is very powerful; surely that can go either way. *Yes,* James says, *it can—but it generally doesn't.* The tongue is not something we tend to use for good. That brings us to the second characteristic of the tongue: its destructiveness. Yes, the tongue can make great boasts, but none of them are good.

Destructive

So far, James has likened the tongue to things that are good, or at the very least, neutral; small things that have enormous impact. But now he shows us what kind of impact our tongues generally have. For this, he turns from horses and ships to fire, and invites us to "consider what a great forest is set on fire by a small spark" (**v 5**).

James is not just throwing this out there as a passing comparison. He tells us to think, to "consider", how forest fires happen. I once saw a bushfire from an aeroplane. Even from 35,000 feet it looked vast, stretching to the horizon in each direction. It is hard to imagine the impact and destruction a fire that large can cause. James wants us to think about how it might have started. A fire of even thousands of acres in size can be started by just one small spark, perhaps from an engine, or a cigarette discarded carelessly. That one spark can wipe out a whole region.

And this, of all images, is the one James uses to illustrate the scale and type of impact our words can have. The tongue is incendiary: "The tongue also is a fire" (**v 6**).

What's Really Going on in Your Mouth...

James provides an anatomy of the tongue, and it is devastating reading.

- It is "a world of evil" (**v 6**). It stands out from all the other parts of the body by this one dreadful distinction. This cannot be said of any other part of the body in the same way. The tongue has a capacity for evil like nothing else. You can't imagine whole sections of the book of Proverbs being taken up with the use and misuse of the elbow or the toe. But the tongue is an entire ecosystem of sin, a world in itself: continents of wickedness, vast uncharted interiors of any number of evils. The potential for any number of world-changing horrors lies right there in your mouth. No wonder John Calvin wrote:

"A slender portion of flesh contains in it the whole world of iniquity." (*James*, page 320)

■ "It corrupts the whole body" (**v 6**). In the tongue's awful capabilities it is unique in the human body, and now we see that it actually affects the whole body. Every other part of the body is unlike it, and yet devastated by it. Every area of life is scorched and charred by its fires. Nothing is beyond its impact. We hear echoes of Jesus' own teaching, that it is "what comes out of their mouth" that defiles someone (Matthew 15:11). Havoc is wreaked everywhere.

■ The tongue "sets the whole course of one's life on fire" (James **3:6**). The totality extends not just to the tongue's reach, but also to its duration. Throughout the whole of life, all the twists and turns and ups and downs, from the cradle to the grave, the tongue blazes away.

The tongue is the one muscle of our bodies that we do not fail to exercise thoroughly. It gets a constant workout. Fire spreads everywhere; sparks are constantly flying out of our mouths, spraying in every direction. A bit of innuendo; a harsh word to our parents or our spouse; sniping to take someone down; some gossip juicily passed on; a dash of exaggeration as we recount something to others. It can all seem so harmless at the time. A spark is such a small thing, after all. And yet "what a great forest is set on fire by a small spark" (**v 5**). Just a few careless words, either deliberate or accidental, and the result can be untold damage. We think of careers that have toppled, marriages that have fallen apart, conflicts that have been started, and decades of self-loathing that have been generated, all because of carelessly uttered words.

I spent a few minutes looking online for information on some of the world's most poisonous creatures. What is amazing is how small many of these creatures are, and how out of all proportion to the size of their likely predators is the strength of poison they carry. Why would such a small jellyfish or spider really need to pack enough poison to drop an elephant? Add to that list our tongues. James says our tongues are "full of deadly poison" (**v 8**). In the search for weapons of mass destruction, we really only need to look in the mirror and open our mouths.

None of this turns out to be surprising when we realise where all this destruction really comes from.

■ It "is … set on fire by hell" (**v 6**). Why, when our tongues have the potential to do untold good as well as untold bad, do they so often seem to incline to wreaking such havoc? James points us to the spark that fuels all other sparks. Our words are so destructive because they are, in actual fact, hellish. If we all speak with the same unpleasant moral accent, it is because all our words hail from exactly the same place. All that spoken fire spewed from all those lives through all history and across the whole world has its origin here. Our tongues are satanic.

Uncontrollable

This is stark stuff. And James isn't finished yet. Next, he takes us to the zoo: "All kinds of animals, birds, reptiles and sea creatures are being tamed and have been tamed by mankind" (**v 7**). We have trained elephants to play football, dolphins to head a ball into a hoop, parrots to sing along to karaoke tracks, dogs to bring us our slippers. Given the right circumstances and time, we seem able to train pretty much any animal to do any task. There are people who have raised lions and tigers to be pets. Animals which would otherwise have a natural propensity to rip a person to shreds in a matter of seconds are happy to snuggle up to their owners and eat out of their hands. It is a marvellous human ability.

But our capacity for taming things is not boundless. Our abilities to tame and to train reach an abrupt halt when we get to our tongues:

"No human being can tame the tongue. It is a restless evil, full of deadly poison" (**v 8**).

It is remarkable. We can do so much, yet we cannot do this little thing. We are reminded of this whenever we see someone powerful brought down by one word that they can't take back; or when we see someone who's made a career of watching what they say finally come undone in just one unguarded moment. Whatever we're able to do with the wildest of beasts, we will never be able to do with the contents of our own mouths. It is simply beyond us. If you think your speech is something you can sort out, you are kidding yourself. However successful and able you are, your tongue will never be something you can conquer yourself.

We need to grasp this or we will misunderstand what James is saying in these verses. He is not outlining a programme for mastering our tongues: *Seven Steps to Flawlessly Controlled Speech*. His aim is precisely the opposite. He is saying: *This is not something you are able to do. You need to, desperately; but you can't.* It is beyond human capacity.

Discouraging as this is, it should not surprise us. The reason the tongue is beyond our control is because of what it is: the outflow of our hearts. And because this is so, this is a very humbling passage. We do well to feel its force and confess to God and ourselves its truth. James has wisdom and help for us in the verses that follow, but we will make no progress unless we first recognise the extent of the problem we have with our tongues.

Questions for reflection

1. How do James' words here prompt and shape your reflection on what you have said to others in the last few days?

2. What did you find most challenging about these verses?

3. Is there a way you have used your tongue, perhaps recently or years ago, that you need to repent of and seek someone's forgiveness for? How will you go about doing that today?

James is continuing with his examination of our tongues, and the news does not get any better. He has already established that the tongue is almost unbelievably powerful, relentlessly destructive, and beyond our capacity to control. He now adds to that unhappy diagnosis that the tongue is revealing; it flawlessly shows what is really going on inside of us.

Revealing

The tongue is something of a spiritual barometer: it shows us what is really going on inside us. We use our words to "praise our Lord and Father"; yet we also use our tongues to "curse human beings, who have been made in God's likeness" (**v 9**). "Out of the same mouth come praise and cursing" (**v 10**). Our tongues show how fundamentally inconsistent we are.

We have already been warned about being double-minded. In the discussion on praying to God for wisdom, James cautioned that those who were being double-minded should not expect to receive it. Being double-minded is trying to think and live in two directions at once—both God's and the world's. It lies behind much of what James says throughout this letter, and this tendency to praise God while cursing some of the people he has made is another example of it.

James's critique is searching. It is easy in Christian meetings, Sunday by Sunday, to sing praises to God. Often, such praise seems heartfelt. We feel as if we mean it. But the problem is that it may only be moments after the meeting that I am speaking against someone—uttering an unfair critical comment, or a piece of gossip. And this is heartfelt, too. Humans have a capacity to delight in God and then to curse someone that God has not only made, but made in his likeness.

What this exposes is a fundamental inconsistency: a love for God, and an antagonism for him that co-exist in us at the same time. "My brothers and sisters, this should not be" (**v 10**). What is being revealed by the tongue no Christian is to be happy with. Wherever this double-mindedness is evident, there needs to be recognition that something is fundamentally wrong. It "should not be". We must never be satisfied with this situation. Yet many of us do not even notice it.

James turns to the natural world to show us just how wrong this state of affairs is: "Can both fresh water and salt water flow from the same spring? My brothers and sisters, can a fig-tree bear olives, or a grapevine bear figs? Neither can a salt spring produce fresh water" (**v 11-12**). As we look at the world, this principle is very clear: a product is always consistent with its source.

> More than anything else, our tongue shows what kind of people we are.

A source of one kind is not going to produce something of two kinds. Fresh and salt water will never flow from the same spring. Fresh water comes from one kind of source; salt water from another. There is no such thing as a blended source that can produce both. The product always matches the source.

The product is therefore always a reflection of the source. What you end up with shows what you started with. Fruit is always in line with its source. If someone wants some fresh olives, it is no use looking for them among the fig trees; fig trees are for figs. And if it's figs you want, there's little point rummaging through the grapevines for them. As carefully as someone might look, they will never find raspberries on an apple tree, or bananas in a field of potato plants.

It is the same when it comes to the tongue. What we say is an issue precisely because it reflects what is going on underneath. The kind of fruit in evidence indicates what kind of tree is producing it. The type of language we speak indicates what kind of heart lies behind it. It shows us what is really going on under the surface. If you want to know what someone is really like, spend time listening to them talk.

More than anything else, the tongue shows what kind of people we are. Douglas Moo sums it up neatly:

"Bad things don't produce good things. And so a person who is not right with God and walking daily in his presence cannot consistently speak pure and helpful words."

(The Letter of James, page 166)

As ever, James is drawing on the teaching of Jesus:

"Make a tree good and its fruit will be good, or make a tree bad and its fruit will be bad, for a tree is recognised by its fruit. You brood of vipers, how can you who are evil say anything good? For the mouth speaks what the heart is full of. A good man brings good things out of the good stored up in him, and an evil man brings evil things out of the evil stored up in him." (Matthew 12:33-35)

To praise God and then speak against someone in his likeness shows what our hearts are truly like. We might sing of our love for him, but the reality is very different. Our other words show us what the truth is. The uncomfortable conclusion is that unChristian speech is evidence of an un-Christian heart.

Impossible for us, but...

James has shown us what our tongues are like: powerful, destructive, uncontrollable, and revealing. How are we to respond? It would be easy to infer from all this that silence is golden. If we have taken James seriously, perhaps there ought to be a thought in each of us that we should endeavour never to say anything ever again. But this is not the right approach. James has already shown us that Christians should expect to exhibit a measure of self-control with their speech, to "keep a tight rein on their tongues" (1:26), to be "never at fault in what they say" (**3:2**). If the tongue is beyond our control, how can this discipline ever be possible?

The answer lies in what follows. What is impossible for man is gloriously possible for God. Our tongues need to be set alight, not from below by hell but from above by God himself.

The Nature of Wisdom

James starts us off with a question: "Who is wise and understanding among you?" (**v 13**). It is a vitally important question. Where is the wisdom and understanding in any given church family? How can we tell? If the church we belonged to suddenly needed a new pastor or extra leadership to be appointed from within, to whom would we look? And what do we base our assessment on when trying to determine who is wise?

A common tendency is to equate wisdom and understanding with cleverness. So we tend to look for the people who seem to know the most, have had the most theological training, or just sound as if they know what they are talking about. But James cautions us against that assumption: "Who is wise and understanding among you? Let them show it by their good life, by deeds done in the humility that comes from wisdom" (**v 13**).

Wisdom is something that can be shown, and does not exist if it is not shown. It is seen—not primarily in words, but in deeds. It is someone's conduct and how they live, rather than their brainpower and what they know, that shows they are wise. James is not writing off the need for knowledge; he is showing us where wisdom is seen. Its evidence is, ultimately, behavioural rather than intellectual.

In looking for wisdom we are to look for the good life, not clever answers. And the good life is one made up of deeds done in humility. Wisdom leads to humility, which in turn produces good deeds.

James mentions this here because it is the answer to the problem of our tongues. The tongue shows us what is going on with the heart, and so the way to deal with the tongue is to deal with the heart beneath it. Change the heart, and the speech will follow. Every wrong form of speech is a sign that there is a lack of wisdom. It is the product of a proud heart that harbours "bitter envy and selfish ambition" (**v 14**). Pride means we want to promote ourselves and bring others down. Pride is nothing to be proud of! A "wisdom" that is motivated by wishing to pull others down or push ourselves forward is the opposite of heavenly: it is "demonic" (**v 15**). Douglas Moo puts it succinctly. False wisdom:

"is the direct antithesis of 'the wisdom that comes from above'— heavenly in nature, spiritual in essence, and divine in origin."

(*The Letter of James,* page 173)

The Source of Wisdom

So how is such wisdom to be gained? Where can you find it? To understand this, we need to see the ways in which real wisdom differs from worldly wisdom.

There are two kinds of wisdom, and they are wildly different. One comes from heaven; the other is earthly. One is spiritual; the other unspiritual. One is from God; the other is from the devil (**v 15**). True wisdom, in other words, comes from outside this world. It comes from God alone, as the Proverb reminds us: "For the LORD gives wisdom; from his mouth come knowledge and understanding" (Proverbs 2:6). And, as James has already told us: "If any of you lacks wisdom, you should ask God" (James 1:5). We cannot gain true wisdom without turning to God for it. If the source of this wisdom is God, we need to be those who pray. The fact is, we need

> To truly know yourself is to know yourself as someone in need of grace.

to have God's perspective on our lives. We need him to humble our hearts. We need him to tame our tongues. It is why humility and wisdom go together in this passage: to truly know yourself is to know yourself as someone in need of God's grace.

The Fruit of Wisdom

Wisdom—true wisdom from above—has effects. Just like faith, it can be seen. It is "first of all pure; then peace-loving, considerate, submissive, full of mercy and good fruit, impartial and sincere" (**3:17**). This is in stark contrast to the "fruit" of the earthly wisdom that James has just described—envious, selfish, leading to disorder and evil (**v 16**). These two wisdoms are not only radically different in their source, but also in their outcome. Pre-eminent among the effects of heavenly wisdom is purity. There is a quality to this kind of knowing that comes from God that sets its recipients apart. This purity is not the musty, stuffy prudishness we so often think of when this word comes to mind. Whereas earthly wisdom produces strife and sets people apart from one another, God's wisdom leads to harmony. Those possessed of it start to love peace more than selfish ambition. There is a consideration of others where once there was one-upmanship and envy. In other words, the purity of God's wisdom shows itself relationally. This is where it is seen.

And this relational peaceableness itself has knock-on effects: "Peacemakers who sow in peace reap a harvest of righteousness" (**v 18**). The behaviour produced by wisdom invests itself in such a way as to lead to further fruit. We should think of this "harvest of righteousness" in two particular regards. First, in our own lives—as we live in the light of the wisdom that God graciously gives his people, we become increasingly pleasing to him in the way we live. We exhibit more and more of it by leading a "good life, by deeds done in the humility that comes from wisdom" (**v 13**)—especially, given the context, in the kind of speech we use.

But second, James must also have in mind an impact beyond our own lives. The language of harvest suggests such an attractive way of life that others are drawn to God through it—a behaviour so compelling that it becomes the clincher for some who are coming to trust in the gospel for the first time. It also suggests an attractive change not just in our deeds but our words.

A Different Fire

There is a wonderful illustration of what James is saying here in the book of Acts on the day of **Pentecost**, when the Holy Spirit was poured out on the early Christian believers.

> "When the day of Pentecost came, they were all together in one place. Suddenly a sound like the blowing of a violent wind came from heaven and filled the whole house where they were sitting. They saw what seemed to be tongues of fire that separated and came to rest on each of them. All of them were filled with the Holy Spirit and began to speak in other tongues as the Spirit enabled them." (Acts 2:1-4)

Notice the connection, once again, between fire and speech. But notice too that in this instance that speech is not set on fire by hell (as in James **3:6**); the tongues of fire come down from heaven and rest on the believers. And because the fire comes from a very different place, it has a very different effect. A different kind of speech is produced; not one that leads to the cursing of those made in God's image, but to the praise of God himself:

> "Now there were staying in Jerusalem God-fearing Jews from every nation under heaven. When they heard this sound, a crowd came together in bewilderment, because each one heard their own language being spoken." (Acts 2:5-6)

It is James 3 in reverse. The effects of the tongue are no less widespread, but now the great forest is ablaze with the Spirit of God. The small spark of gospel living is able to change the course of a whole life and even whole communities and nations.

Such godly fire only comes from heaven by the Spirit of God. If we

Heavenly speech is now our native tongue, and we need to learn fluency.

have come to Christ, this new kind of speech is now our native tongue. We need to learn fluency, praying for this aspect of the Spirit's work in our lives so that he might take our tongues and use them to God's glory. Knowing that this new kind of speech is possible gives us spiritual confidence where once we would have lacked it. The believer is not instructed in the New Testament to silence their tongue, but to use it. Our conversation is to be filled with the grace of God and seasoned with the salt of the gospel (Colossians 4:5-6). We are to be poised and ready to give an account of the hope that we have (1 Peter 3:15).

Questions for reflection

1. What does *your* tongue reveal about *your* heart?

2. How does thinking about our use of words cause you to adore Jesus even more for the way he used his own tongue?

3. In what practical ways will you make every effort, prayerfully, to speak more fluently in your "native tongue" today?

7. COMING BACK TO GOD

Conflict is part of everyday life, and comes in all sorts of contexts. It might be a blow-up at home or work, with friends or with strangers. And it can take various forms. There is the conflict that's a very obvious falling out; there is the quiet, unspoken animosity that can exist for years under the veneer of friendship (or even marriage); there is conflict that hurts and scars deeply; and there is the sort that might not even be recognised, because for one side it is just a minor spat, while for the other it is a huge deal. Some carry the bruising because of wounds they have received; others carry guilt because of the damage they know they've done to others.

Conflict does not cease at the door of the church. The battles that are part of life in the world can sadly just as easily be part of life in the church. Any two individuals have the potential for conflict. It can be just as common for the Christian—sometimes, it seems, even more common for the Christian—and no less painful. Conflict in the church is often hidden. Christians do not commonly resort to fists, but they don't need to; James has already shown us that we carry in our mouths a weapon far more destructive.

The new Christian might be shocked by the conflict that can be part and parcel of church life. They are right to be. Christians should be different. James insists we can be, and calls on us to take the necessary steps to prevent conflict among God's people.

The Cause of Conflict

James begins by asking another of his penetrating questions: "What causes fights and quarrels among you?" (James **4:1**). He invites his readers to cast their minds back to some recent conflict. What happened? Why did it take place? If there is a conflict that seems to keep recurring, why does it do so? What is going on?

When we think of times when things have flared up with someone else, our instinct often is to answer James' question in a particular way. What is the cause of a fight or quarrel with this other party? *They are!* If they weren't so unreasonable, or demanding, or if they were more thoughtful and considerate, then there would be no problem! The answer seems obvious: other people are to blame for our conflicts.

However much we might want to, James won't let us answer the question in that way. The issue is not everybody else, but us. The problem is not out there; it is in here—in us.

James has had to point us to the true nature of our hearts already. It is from the evil desires of our own hearts that temptation comes (1:14). It is the state of our own hearts that is reflected in the godless speech that too often characterises us (3:9-12). It is no surprise, then, that James would point to these same desires in order to get to the root of our conflicts. Our fights and quarrels stem "from your desires that battle within you ... You desire but you do not have, so you kill. You covet but you cannot get what you want, so you quarrel and fight" (**4:1-2**).

Conflict comes because our own selfish desires are not being met. James uses strong language; we might think he is being over the top—after all, we don't literally kill one another. But as James' older brother (Jesus) once pointed out (Matthew 5:21-22), we do not need to kill in order to commit a form of murder.

So to understand conflict, we need to understand the desires jostling within us that are being frustrated. It might be the desire for status that leads us to vie for positions of influence and to envy others and do them down. It might be a desire to get even with someone who has hurt us, and so bitterness is nurtured over months and years. Or it could be the desire to protect ourselves from criticism that causes us to lash out at others pre-emptively. But whatever they are, underlying all these selfish desires is lack of proper thinking about God.

Don't Ask, Don't Get

Christians allowing these desires to erupt into conflict are forgetting God's grace: "You do not have because you do not ask God" (James **4:2b**). Prayerlessness is a sign that someone is trying to run things in their own strength, for their own sake, and under their own authority. Prayerlessness arises from a sense of independence from God—so that instead of praying about our desires, we indulge them. Rather than trusting in the Father, who delights in giving good gifts to his children (Matthew 7:11), we ourselves decide what is good and seek to gain it through our own efforts.

As well as forgetting the grace of God, James' readers also forget the goodness of God: "When you ask, you do not receive, because you ask with wrong motives, that you may spend what you get on your pleasures" (James **4:3**). God is utterly pure—his eyes are too pure to look on evil (Habakkuk 1:13). But James rebukes his readers for only turning to God so that he can rubber-stamp their own agenda, rather than submitting to his. This is a huge misunderstanding of what prayer is for. Think about the Lord's Prayer (see Matthew 6:9-13). When Jesus taught his disciples to pray, he pointed them to pray for God's concerns (his name, his kingdom, his will) before our own (of provision, pardon and protection). The purpose of prayer is not to try to get God to do what we want; it is actually a means by which we align ourselves to his priorities. Part of the point of prayer is to remind ourselves of what God wants.

But for many of James' readers, prayer seems to have been a means of co-opting God into their plans—of using him to further their own purposes. Little wonder, then, that they did not receive the things they prayed for. As the British pastor and evangelist Rico Tice puts it:

"We turn God into a divine waiter. He is there to deliver our day-dream to us. We touch base with him on a Sunday; we put our order in via prayer; we might give a decent tip in the collection plate. But God is essentially there to give us what we feel we need … and we get furious with him if he doesn't deliver."

(*Honest Evangelism*, page 43)

When we allow the desires of our own hearts to grow unchecked, the result is a lack of answers to prayer—either because we become so engrossed in achieving our goals by our own means (and so do not come to God in prayer at all), or because we come to God treating him as the means to our own ends (and therefore praying with ungodly motives and intentions). If you don't see many answers to your prayers, maybe the problem is with your prayers!

The key to living authentically as Christians is to think rightly about God.

Once again, James is showing us that key to living authentically as Christians is to think rightly about God. The presence of conflicts between Christians is a sign that God's grace and goodness are not at the forefront of his people's thinking. Time and again, as he addresses the problems being faced by his readers, James turns their attention to what God is like. This is a reminder to us that real theology (how we understand and think about God) is essentially practical. Who we understand God to be shapes the way we live. Far from being a distraction from day-to-day Christian living, the doctrine of God is the key to it. Without it the church becomes prayerless, joyless, fractious and selfish.

It is the grace and goodness of God that spurs the church not just to pray, but to pray with motivations that honour God. It is the proper response to the selfish desires within our hearts that so easily bring us into conflict.

Adulterous Hearts

Our selfish desires lead to conflict with one another; they also lead to a more serious conflict—one with God. The conflict between us that shows we have selfish hearts is also a sign that we have adulterous hearts. Spiritually, we are unfaithful to God. Just pause to consider that accusation. James is not pulling any punches: "You adulterous people, don't you know that friendship with the world means enmity against God? Therefore, anyone who chooses to be a friend of the world becomes an enemy of God" (James **4:4**).

The imagery here is powerful. We are to think of the horror of a husband or wife discovering their spouse in the midst of an affair. James says that such horrendous behaviour aptly describes what Christians do when they turn their back on God. This marital language is not original to James; the Old Testament commonly speaks of God coming to his people as a husband comes to his bride, and of his people responding in unfaithfulness to him. Christians two-time God when we adopt the values of the world.

James has shown us that if we look inside ourselves, we see selfish hearts. This is true of the whole world. The default setting for all people is to live with themselves at the centre. Ever since the first sin of Adam and Eve in the Garden of Eden, this is what comes naturally to us. It is the very mentality for which we need forgiveness, for it pushes God from his rightful place. When Christians adopt this mindset, they are figuratively climbing back into bed with the world. It is not friendship with people in the world that's wrong, but friendship with the values of the world. And God takes it personally—just like a husband who finds his wife back in bed with the thug she was dating before he had come into her life and rescued her from that awful relationship. Such a husband would have every right to be angry. And James is very clear that being unfaithful to God provokes his enmity.

Most people experience some form of opposition in their lives. It might be the competitive colleague at work vying for the boss's approval or the promotion; or the long-term hostility of someone with whom there has been a falling out; or even as serious as another person intent on causing as much harm and pain as possible. Opposition—in any form—is an awful reality. But James raises the prospect of something far more horrifying: provoking the opposition of God himself. Our selfish desires point to an unfaithfulness to God which puts us on a collision course with him.

James gives us a simple equation: friendship with the world = enmity with God (**v 4**). In other words, the health of our relationship with God is quickly established by examining the desires in our hearts: are they godly, or worldly? Do we chase the things the world chases, or are our deepest desires for the things of God—his reputation, the good of his people, and service of others?

God, James says, is a jealous God (**v 5**). Again, James is using marital imagery. He is jealous for us in the same way a jilted husband is jealous for his wife. God is deserving of our all: "Or do you think Scripture says without reason that he jealously longs for the spirit he has caused to dwell in us?" (**v 5**).

This is a difficult verse to translate. It might be that by his Spirit God is jealous, or that he jealously longs for our spirit—our inner self—to be devoted. Either way, his concern and longing is that those who have wandered would return. The state of unfaithfulness that some of James' readers (and perhaps some of us right now) have got themselves into needs to end. It is time for those who have been captured by the values and priorities of the world to come back to their God.

And wonderfully, "he gives us more grace. That is why Scripture says: 'God opposes the proud but shows favour to the humble'" (**v 6**).

> Will love of self draw me from God, or will love of God draw me from myself?

God wants his people back. Amazingly, God will take his people back. God finds us in bed with the world; yet he still wants us back, so that we might enjoy the blessing of life with him. And so each of us is faced with a choice: will love of self draw me from God, or will love of God draw me from myself? Will we invite God's opposition, or receive his grace? There is no third option—no neutral place. We are either friends with the world, or friends with God. We cannot pursue both.

James is calling on us to acknowledge our guilt before God. The conflicts we experience within the community of his people indicate that selfish desires are lying at the heart of our churches. The selfishness of the world is setting the agenda, and there is hostility between Christians, and a lack of prayerful intimacy with God. Worldly desires reflect a worldly attitude, one which is intolerable to the God who has purchased his people for himself.

Our first step in finding the remedy to this situation is acknowledging how we have come to be in it. We need to admit what is going on in our hearts, and how that has affected our relationship with God, and our relationship with others. We need to come back. We need his grace. Wonderfully, he gives it.

Questions for reflection

1. Consider a conflict you have been involved in. What did it reveal about your heart? How did it affect your prayers?

2. How does verse 4 cause you to take your sin more seriously?

3. Meditate on the great truth of verse 6: "He gives us more grace". Why is that truth particularly precious to you today?

PART TWO

James has just been calling on his readers to return to God. He now unpacks what that will look like. Wonderfully, he shows us there is grace for those who submit to God. But the grace that forgives is also grace that changes and transforms people. James offers no lip-service Christianity. It is not possible to jump on board, receive blessings from God, and then run straight back into the old lifestyle. God's grace prompts repentance in his people—a heart change that will lead to transformed behaviour.

Our Dealings with God

The remedy to our pride and worldliness is to submit to God: "Submit yourselves, then, to God" (**v 7**). Submitting to God is yielding to him, recognising his just and rightful rule over our lives.

And submission is not an optional extra to the Christian life, as though the main business of being in relationship with him is somehow unrelated to submission, or as though submission only occasionally needs to come into play. Submitting to God is part of what it means to relate rightly to him. When Jesus addressed those who wanted to be his disciples, he told them they must: "Deny themselves and take up their cross daily and follow me" (Luke 9:23). By calling the worldly Christian to submit, James is calling them back to what the Christian life should always be marked by.

But submission is especially appropriate in this context. Our conflicts, we've seen, are the result of our godless desires not being indulged. So the answer is found in submitting our desires to him, giving them over to him, and even asking him not to give us the things we deeply want when the things we deeply want are selfish.

This is straightforward to understand, but very hard to do. By definition, our desires are rooted deep within us, and are not going to be resisted or transformed without difficulty. Even as we start to think of what might need to be involved, even as we identify specific and long-standing desires that need to be yielded to God, we sense a deep resistance to letting go of them, a force pushing back against us as we try to submit to God. As we see a desire that is ungodly, and think: *That needs working on*, we find the thought changes to: *That probably needs working on at some point, but not right now.* Or: *It's not the most important thing in the world. I'll think about it another time. This doesn't need to be done today.*

This is why James moves immediately to teachings about the devil. The Bible is clear that the devil is a real force in the world. Many of our questions about where he came from and what he is like the Bible does not fully answer for us. As with so many issues of the Christian life, we are told what we need to know rather than everything we would like to know. And a significant part of what we Christians need to know is that we are to "resist the devil" (James **4:7**).

To resist the devil does not mean that we blame him for the times when we follow our own desires. We need to acknowledge his influence and do all we can to resist him. We need to determine not to be taken in by his lies, not to indulge our own pride. And as we resist him, James says something wonderful will happen: "He will flee from you" (**v 7**).

We see here a wonderful biblical balance. We are to be mindful of the devil's existence and of his ways of working against the people of God. Peter reminds us that the devil is our "enemy" and "prowls around like a roaring lion looking for someone to devour" (1 Peter 5:8). It would be a fatal folly to ignore him and his ways. He is real, and so are

> The devil is not to be ignored or trivialised, nor unduly feared.

his destructive intentions towards us. Removing him entirely from our consideration will leave us all the more vulnerable and susceptible to his attacks. Sticking your head in the sand in the presence of a lion may dull the sound of his roaring, but does little to lessen your chances of being devoured. The devil is to be neither ignored nor trivialised—but nor is he to be unduly feared.

James is unequivocal: as we resist the devil, he will flee (James **4:7**). We are to be aware of him (how else could we resist him?), but we are not to spend our Christian lives cowering in fear of what he might do next. More than anything else, the devil longs for us to betray our loyalty to God, to follow him in the path of disobedience. Hence the coupling together of our resistance to the devil and our submission to God; the highest form of resistance to the devil is to submit all that we are to our true King. Nothing will cause greater upset to the devil's schemes than our willing, joyful submission to God. As we submit to God, we by definition resist the devil. And we can only resist the devil as we submit to God. That is what we must strive to do. Such a fight puts him to flight.

Many of us will have encountered bullies in life. It may have been in the school classroom or playground, or the adult-life equivalents that are common in the offices and homes of this world. In the face of aggression and greater strength, it is all too easy to be intimidated. But imagine a bully who you knew would flee the moment you stood up to him! We would not take long to learn that we needn't feel intimidated or live in fear. However powerful and fearful a force the devil is, we can be assured that our resistance will not be futile. Our tendency is to be drawn into conflict with one another; James would have us fight the devil, not each other.

To resist the devil is to turn towards God. And James could give us no greater encouragement to do so than this: when we draw near to God, he draws near to us—as you "come near to God … he will come near to you" (**v 8a**). This is not to deny that God is the one to make the first move towards us in securing our forgiveness. In the Bible, God is always the one to initiate relationship—*always*. James is talking here about Christians turning back to God in repentance, having drifted away from him. When we do so, we will find that God is not reluctant to embrace us. The **prodigal son** found he had barely breasted the horizon on his way home when his father ran to him. He had hardly started his rehearsed words of repentance before finding fatherly arms gripping him tightly (Luke 15:20-24). Wonderfully, however much or far we have strayed, we can know that when we truly come back to God, we find our relationship restored.

But turning to God must involve turning from sin. The prodigal son did not find restored relationship with his father while he remained lying in his pigsty. We are told: "Wash your hands, you sinners, and purify your hearts, you double-minded" (James **4:8b**). Notice repentance involves both hands and heart, actions and attitude, behaviour and mindset. It must always be so. Repentance of attitude without change in conduct is no repentance at all. Nor can we expect to change our behaviour without seriously changing the thoughts and attitudes that lie behind it. Repentance must involve both hands and heart. Each is in need of change, for it is with both that we stray from God. Just as real faith acts, so real repentance changes.

A Life of Joyful Grief

What does this turn from sin look like? "Grieve, mourn and wail. Change your laughter to mourning and your joy to gloom" (**v 9**). These are very strong words. We need to be clear both about what James means, and what he doesn't mean. James is *not* saying there is no place for joy and laughter in the Christian life. That would be nonsense, for he has already told us to "consider it pure joy" when we face trials (1:2). There is joy and laughter to be found even in a hurting world, if we know the God who rules and guides all things and who works for his children's good as he does so (Romans 8:28).

But there is a place for seriousness and grief about sin. In fact, this goes hand in hand with our joy in Christ. The more we know of him, the more horrific we realise our sin to be. It is not some trivial thing that God can just sweep under the carpet; it cost no less than the blood of Jesus. It is not something God will merely wink at and brush aside. The cross that stands at the heart of our faith is testament to the fact that sin is deserving of the very wrath of God—a wrath that the Son was willing to bear on our behalf, and a wrath whose awfulness we see as he cried out of his forsakenness on that cross. The more we understand this, the deeper should be our sense of grief whenever we find ourselves caught in sin. Sin should be something we mourn. It is right to weep over it.

I was catching up with a great friend recently. We both observed that we cry more easily than we used to, and reckoned this was probably a good thing overall. But the fact is I am often more easily moved to tears by Pixar movies, mushy adverts and friends' weddings than I am by my sin. So these words of James are a challenge. We are not just to regret our sin, but to grieve over it. If we are not more emotional over our sin (and our salvation) than we are over our sports team's successes or failures, the plot twists in our favourite films, our children's achievements or disappointments, and so on, then there is something wrong—and that something is that we do not appreciate what our sin is, and what it cost our Saviour to rescue us from it. Sin is not cheap.

> There should be no people more sad, and yet more happy, than Christians.

It is only as we recognise who we are—sinners—and grieve over that truth, that we discover what it means for God to draw near to us: "Humble yourselves before the Lord, and he will lift you up" (James **4:10**). Godly grief over sin is where our repentance must begin; but it is not where God leaves us. Gloom and grief are part of the genuine Christian response to sin, but they are not the totality of our Christian experience. God humbles us not to keep us down, but to lift us up. It is the contrite in heart that God esteems (Isaiah 66:2), and the poor in spirit who receive the kingdom of heaven (Matthew 5:3). Complacent laughter gives way to mourning, and mourning now gives way to the joy of our salvation. There should be no people more sad, and yet more happy, than Christians. The lower we are, the more lifted we are. It is the great paradox of the Christian life that we weep over our sin while singing in astounded joy of our salvation.

Our Dealings with One Another

James now takes us to the second dimension of our repentance: from the vertical to the horizontal. Our repentance and salvation have practical outworkings, and here he tells us not to "slander one another" (James **4:11**). It is all too easy to speak against others. James has shown us why this is—our tongues are untamed and are, in our own strength, untameable. Running others down in what we say is so reflexive that we barely even know we are doing it. So we need to train ourselves to think differently about what we say.

James shows us that to speak against another is to "[speak] against the law" (**v 11**). The law, after all, calls on us to love our neighbour as ourselves, and not to judge them or to trample all over them to fulfil our own desires. When we do so, we exempt ourselves from God's law. We say, in effect, that it doesn't apply to our treatment of this person in this situation, that we are excused from its obligations, and that in this instance we know better than God does. We sit in judgment over it, deciding if and when and how it comes into effect for us.

So we cannot slander the law without slandering God. He, after all, is the Lawmaker and the Lawgiver. To put ourselves above his laws and his demands is to put ourselves above him—it is to repeat the first sin in Eden (Genesis 3:1-7). When we decide we know better than his law, we decide we know better than him—that it's justified to act this way even when he says not to. We end up playing God. We forget who he is, and who we are. And "there is only one Lawgiver and judge" (James **4:12**). Worse, rejecting him and appointing ourselves in his place means rejecting the only one "who is able to save" us from himself and the destruction he visits upon those who turn away from life with and blessing from him (**v 12**).

How we treat others reflects our view of who God is. He alone has the right to show us how to live and behave with others. He is the one who will judge justly, who can save and destroy—not us. Our behaviour towards others is to be determined by him and his law, and not by our own selfish desires and wants. If we find ourselves in the sort of conflicts with one another that marked James' readers, then it means we're not submitting to God. Not really. True submission to God humbles us; it reminds us of who we are—and it reminds us of who we're not. How often we forget the simple truth: you're not God! And when we do, we are unable to appreciate the wonderful truth: you are ruled by and saved by God. Essential to knowing who you are is knowing whose you are.

Questions for reflection

1. Use the aspects of genuine repentance that James lays out in verses 7-10 in your own prayers of repentance now.

2. "How we treat others reflects our view of who God is." What does this truth say about you and your faith?

3. "He will lift you up" (v 10). How does this passage move you to appreciate the grace of God even more than you did yesterday?

8. ON SCHEDULES AND BANK BALANCES

One of the features of the church is its diversity. The gospel can and should bring together people who would otherwise be worlds apart. But this feature can just as easily be a problem. Where there are differences, there will be comparisons. Comparisons often lead to judgments, and judgments to divisions.

This is perhaps especially true when the differences among God's people are economic. If you have richer and poorer people together in the same place, life will never be the same again. There is the potential for great tension and division. Economic differences never go unnoticed. So if we are to avoid conflict (the issue James has been addressing since 3:13) we will need to think in godly ways about wealth. James helps us by addressing different groups of people.

A Rebuke to the Arrogant

James begins by addressing travelling merchants: "Now listen, you who say, 'Today or tomorrow we will go to this or that city, spend a year there, carry on business and make money'" (**4:13**). Merchants in James' day would have spent time in a new place, establishing contacts and trading before moving on somewhere else. Then and now, this is the familiar language of everyday planning. The details may differ, but the mentality is much the same. Plans like these are part and parcel of life, and not just for travelling merchants. Whether in full-time employment or not, whether young or old, we need to plan, and to think a year or so ahead. There is nothing wrong with an entrepreneurial spirit. The Bible even commends it (see, for example, Ecclesiastes 9:9-10; Colossians 3:23-24 and Proverbs 12:11).

Such planning is unavoidable in the modern world. Most of us would not be able to function without a diary. Our ever busier lifestyle means we have multiple commitments. Schedules need to be synced, between our own devices and between those of our households. Our time fills up quickly. We need to plan to honour our various home-life and work-life commitments.

Yet in all this busyness and planning, there is a danger: that we adopt an attitude that is ungodly and, in fact, arrogant. To avoid this, James says we need to get two things right.

> We know where we will be in a million years; but we don't know what will happen tomorrow.

First, our view of the future. James (as ever!) cuts to the chase. We "do not even know what will happen tomorrow" (**v 14a**). James puts his finger on an uncomfortable truth: we don't know what the future holds. We've no idea. As Christians, we know where we will be in a million years. That is in God's hands and he's told us about it. But we don't know what will happen tomorrow. That is in God's hands, but he hasn't told us about it. We're in the dark.

On one level we recognise this. We check the traffic reports and the weather forecasts but we know they may have it wrong. We allow for contingencies, and make back-up plans. But on another level, this is something we don't like to think much about. It reminds us that we are not in control. You may not finish reading this chapter before the Lord returns or you breathe your last. That is a profoundly unsettling thought, and one we unconsciously tend to think is best avoided!

And so we tend to plan our lives as if we were in control. We put all our arrangements into the diary as if they were a given: the business trip, the family holiday, the weekend seeing friends, the hours we'll put in at the office, the projects we'll take on; everything from house-work to homework is not just planned, it is assumed. Our default view is that once we plan something, it will happen. James throws a cup of cold water in our faces. We don't know what will happen. None of us do. We need to factor that into our view of the future.

Second, James looks at our view of ourselves. We've seen al-ready that James asks the most penetrating of questions. Here we go with another: "What is your life? You are a mist that appears for a little while and then vanishes" (**v 14b**). As we plan out our lives, carefully shaping our work lives, home lives and social lives, there's a danger that we think we are at the centre of it all. After all, we play the starring role in our diaries. If my life is the *Movie of Me*, then the diary is akin to the screenplay. James has already filled another cup and is swinging it in our direction… *What is your life?* he says. *Well, what is it?* If someone was to write your biography (and that's an idea we'll entertain all too readily), what would you think the title should be?

As I write, it is the Christmas season, and so bookshops are groaning with celebrity autobiographies. Evidently, becoming fa-mous is deemed worthy of being a great story. I imagine that the thought process that goes into coming up with the title is not an edifying one.

James has a very different kind of suggestion. Here's his title for the book that sums up your life, that draws together all your greatest moments and lists your achievements: *Mist*. Fleeting. Around for a few brief moments and then gone without a trace. In the bathroom this morning, the steam from my shower fogged up the mirror. So what did I do? I opened the window, let in a breeze of wintry air and within a few moments, a few mere moments, the steam had com-pletely gone. When I got into my car, the windscreen had misted up with the morning frost. A quick blast from the heater and all was clear again. Had I not been writing this chapter, I would not have thought of the fog on my mirror or the mist on my windscreen again. This is the nature of mist. It goes, and it goes quickly. It is around for a bit and then it's vanished. There's the strapline for your biography: *Appeared for a while, and then vanished.*

Mist. This, of all that James could have called to mind, is what sums up our lives. We are here for a little while, and then we're gone. Yet we plan as if everything we do is terribly significant. Our holidays, our work trips, our gap-year travels. At the moment I'm in the process of planning a sabbatical for next year. My head is full of possibilities: places to visit, projects to work on, and friends to see. Plans are beginning to form. Three or four months that revolve around me. I must be terribly important.

The British evangelist Rico Tice once asked an audience to raise their hands if they knew their great-grandfather's first name. Very few hands went up, from a group of several hundred. Yet, Rico explained, this was a man who was around not many decades ago, whose blood was coursing through their veins, and yet who was already largely forgotten and unknown. Our lives are fleeting; it will not be many years before we are forgotten even by our own family. The world moves on real quick.

In contrast to these wrong views of ourselves and of the future, James offers a different perspective. We should be saying: "If it is the Lord's will, we will live and do this or that" (**v 15**). It would be easy to treat this as if it were just a matter of reciting a formula: mindlessly repeating "If it is the Lord's will" whenever discussing plans or making entries into the diary. No—godliness is far more than sloganeering. James is looking for more than us just tacking a phrase onto our conversation but otherwise carrying on as we were before. As Blomberg and Kamell write:

> "[This] should be interpreted neither as a pious **addendum** to be repeated mindlessly nor as an expression of fatalism that excuses us from taking responsibility for our actions." (*James*, page 209)

It is our attitude that needs to change; our double-mindedness that needs to be repented of.

James is not against planning; he is warning us against planning that does not acknowledge the Lord's sovereign overruling of our lives. The godly response is to plan in a way that recognises and remembers we are not in ultimate control, and that all we plan and conceive is subject to the will of God. He is sovereign; we (for all our busy planning) are not. Our attitude is to be one that is informed and shaped by this reality. All we do is in the hands of God. "In their hearts humans plan their course, but the LORD establishes their steps" (Proverbs 16:9). I am not the master of my own destiny, the captain of my soul. My life is not the unchanging centre of the universe. I am like fleeting mist, and I am not in control of the wind's direction, nor of when I vanish.

What as well as How

This reality affects more than just *how* we plan; it also needs to shape *what* we plan. Not just the contingency but the content of our plans needs to reflect the sovereign rule of God. The 24 hours in the day are not mine to use as I please. God has given them to me, and I am to use them as he would want me to. The plans I form need to reflect this. It is hard to miss the fact that in the example of planning which James has just given us, the planner's bottom line and main aim is making money: "Today or tomorrow we will go to this or that city, spend a year there, carry on business *and make money*" (James **4:13**). Profit is the priority that drives the planning. It is not that making money is bad. It is what merchants do, after all. We would expect nothing different. But this is the point. If our planning is no different to that of the world around us, what does that say about our faith in Christ? It is not wrong for making some money to be a goal in life—we are to support ourselves and help others. But it is wrong for it to be our main goal in life. Our plans need to reflect not only the existence of God's will, but its content too.

In the light of this, the planning that at first seemed innocuous and sensible now starts to sound more than a little vain. These plans are "arrogant schemes"—they are, in fact, "boasting" and "evil" (**v 16**). They have an arrogant view of the future, and of self. They forget God's sovereignty and take no account of God's will.

Planning can so easily be little more than arrogant hot air; we strut and swagger as if we really were something significant. For all our profession of Christian faith, once the calendars come out it is as if God is no longer there. When it comes to planning, we can so quickly become atheists. Our planning revolves around us; our self-important agendas are uppermost in our thinking.

> When it comes to planning, we can so quickly become atheists.

But if we know God, we should know the good we should be doing. God has shown it to us. To say at that point: "My schedule's full" is sin, says James in **verse 17**: to not make time and space for "the good [we] ought to do ... is sin".

What does this look like in reality? It might be that we're becoming more and more irregular in our church attendance. We're not making meeting with God's people a priority. Things are just too busy, we say. "Life's a bit manic at the moment." Or maybe we're not spending time in daily prayer or Bible study, consciously enjoying the presence of God. "I've got too many other things going on at the moment. Maybe when things calm down a bit..." Or perhaps we know deep down that we're not serving the people God has placed around us as we ought to be. Our spouse and kids are getting the bare scraps of our time. Whatever it is, it reflects sin in our planning. We've already made something else our priority and planned around that. We have not reflected on God's will. We are not being driven by what matters most to him, but by what matters most to us. Once again, our worldly desires have exposed the shallowness of our faith. By the time we try to fit some "Christian stuff" in, there's no room for it. And so when we're self-importantly talking about our next big business trip or holiday with the kids, all that's coming out of our mouth is evil boasting about arrogant schemes. The good we ought to be doing is left undone. And that state of affairs is sin.

We are not to eschew planning, nor are we to demonise making money. But what we are to do, James says, is to acknowledge the will of God and to allow that to put our lives, plans and priorities in perspective. That is far easier said than done—but done it must be.

Questions for reflection

1. How can you consciously take account of who you are and who God is in your planning?

2. Are there ways in which your plans don't really reflect God's will? What needs to change?

3. Why is it great news that God is in control of the future?

PART TWO

You Rich People

We know from this letter already that there were enormous tensions between the rich and the poor for James' readers. Many Christians at this time were poor, and being exploited by the rich (2:6-7). In this next section James addresses "you rich people" directly (**5:1**), in some of the strongest language found anywhere in the New Testament.

The first thing we need to do is establish exactly which wealthy people James has in mind in this passage. Rather than addressing the rich in general without distinction, there are good reasons for thinking that James has his sights on the non-Christian rich of his day.

First, at no point anywhere in this passage are these people addressed as "brothers and sisters" or "fellow believers", terms which James has used liberally and consistently through this letter when addressing his Christian readers (eg: 1:16; 2:1, 14; 3:1; 4:11). Second, there is no call to repentance. All we have is unremitting condemnation and the promise of judgment. God's message here is one simply of denunciation. Throughout the letter, even when James has been exposing serious sin in his readers, there has been a constant call to repent and return to wholehearted faith. It is, in fact, the main purpose of the letter: James calling on his readers to turn from sin, and for them to be calling on each other to do so (as we'll see in 5:19-20).

But why would James address the unbelieving rich in this way? They are not the recipients of this letter, and would not be likely to come across it. Why go to all the trouble of crafting such a powerful broadside if it will never reach its target?

James' purpose here is not primarily to teach the ungodly rich about the error of their ways, but to show his Christian readers on the receiving end of their ungodliness what God thinks of it. He wants them to overhear what God would (and will) say to the rich who are giving them such a hard time. If that sounds a rather strange way to proceed, it may help to remember that this was a common **rhetorical**

device in the Old Testament. New Testament scholar Douglas Moo notes that:

"James's style is that of the prophets pronouncing doom on pagan nations. He unrelievedly attacks these people, with no hint of **exhortation**." (*The Letter of James*, page 210)

The people of God in Israel were frequently given prophecies directed to the surrounding nations. The point was not that Isaiah, for example, was about to embark on a preaching tour of these countries and would actually deliver these messages to them, still less that God's people were to take it upon themselves to pass them on. The point was that God's people needed to know what God thought of these people. Doing so would enable the Israelites to know how to think about them themselves. Hearing these **oracles** would show Israel why they were neither to fear nor copy those around them.

James wants his readers to know how to think of the rich people around them. It would be easy to envy them, or to aspire to be like them, or grow bitter that they are not like them. In fact, James shows us in this passage that it is incredibly dangerous to be in the particular position that these rich people find themselves in. So the text is a warning not to head in that direction. As Calvin put it:

> It is not wealth that is the issue, but rather what is done, and not done, with that wealth.

"[James] has a regard to the faithful, that they, hearing of the miserable end of the rich, might not envy their fortune." (*James*, page 342)

So James begins his denunciation on these particular rich people. They ought to "weep and wail because of the misery that is coming on [them]" (**v 1**). The verses that follow explain what it is they're being judged for. It is not wealth that is the issue, but rather, what is done, and not done, with that wealth. James highlights three particular sinful traits; and as we go through them, it is important for us to check ourselves against them too.

Hoarding

> "Your wealth has rotted, and moths have eaten your clothes. Your gold and silver are corroded. Their corrosion will testify against you and eat your flesh like fire. You have hoarded wealth in the last days." (**v 2-3**)

This is a picture of massive waste, of lavish possessions left to rot, like luxury foods that have never been eaten and now never will be. Clothing has become moth-eaten. Expensive jewellery has corroded. All of it was amassed for its own sake. The owner, it seems, never wanted to use it; they just wanted to have it. And now all of it is good for no one. Calvin reminds us of the gravity of this situation:

> "God has not appointed gold for rust, nor garments for moths; but on the contrary, he has designed them as aids and helps to human life." (*James*, page 344)

This is a hugely important warning for those of us living in the West. We live in a society where accumulation is seen as good in its own right. Amassing money and possessions is commended. It is one of the ways that we as a culture measure someone's success in life. The more you have, the better you've done. The things we have are a matter of pride to many of us.

James shows us that to pursue wealth just for its own sake is ungodly. What is wasted "testifies against" us (**v 3**), for it exposes the sinfulness of the human heart that needlessly acquired it all. Hoarding is also foolish, for wealth does not last. Like the material James is describing, it corrodes, rots, and disappears. Our own more sophisticated forms of wealth are no less fickle. It may just take one sharp and sudden downturn in the market. It is the nature of moths to eat clothing and of gold and silver to corrode. This doesn't mean we shun the good things of this world, but it does mean we do not put great stock in them. They are, like us, fleeting. Hoarding for its own sake is very foolish.

This is not to say that Christians are wrong to save for the future, or to contribute to pension plans. But we need to think about the way in which such things are done. As James has just shown us, we do not know the future. All we plan is subject to, and should reflect, the will of God. We also need to think of why we save. Saving is not ungodly if it is for a godly purpose, such as providing for ourselves so that we are not a burden on others, and providing for others. Wealth is to be used, not amassed.

By adding "in the last days" (**v 3**), James also reminds us that the day of reckoning is coming. In the light of God's eternal judgment, the folly of living for possessions in the here and now will be tragically clear for all to see.

Extravagance

"You have lived on the earth in luxury and self-indulgence. You
have fattened yourselves in the day of slaughter." (**v 5**)

James is not saying we cannot enjoy the good things of this world that God gives us (1 Timothy 4:1-5)—that is a denial of the goodness of our Creator God and of what he has made. James is talking about an ungodly attitude that sees ourselves as the centre of everything. The goal in such a life will be to pamper ourselves, going for the most lavish lifestyle we could possibly lead. But, as with all good things, wealth is to be used in the service of others, not in the service of self. Wealth is to be used. We're to be those who have in order to be those who give. In other words, we should never be living as well as we could. Unless we are living right on the poverty line, we should be giving to help meet the needs of others.

So we must not envy the rich their extravagance, whether the rich down the road or the mega-rich in the media. Once again, James reminds us that there is a judgment to come, and for the extravagant it will be a "day of slaughter" (James **5:5**).

Just a couple of miles from where I live is a turkey farm. It is idyllic: surrounded by beautiful countryside, with as much space, fresh air and food as a turkey could need. As far as the turkeys are concerned, this is luxury (as is evidenced by the price they finally reach). Walking past the fence in October, the place is full of plump, happy-looking turkeys. But come the start of January, the same fields are empty. They had feasted in luxury, but all the while they were preparing for the day of slaughter (or Christmas, as we happen to call it). James is saying to the rich people he is addressing here: *You are making the same mistake.*

Injustice

"Look! The wages you failed to pay the workers who mowed your fields are crying out against you. The cries of the harvesters have reached the ears of the Lord Almighty." (**v 4**)

We may not be negligent landowners, as these people evidently were, but this still hits home. It is all too easy for the wealthy to overlook the needs of others and their responsibility to them. For the workmen in the field, a day's wages is everything. No wages means no food for the family. It is a disaster. But for the rich, that wage is just one small detail among many, and therefore easily forgotten. The workman in the fields is just one of the little people. He's just "the help"; paying his wages is an annoying chore. Affluence can lead to carelessness and insensitivity.

But God is concerned for the poor and the oppressed. Through-out the Old Testament he instituted laws to protect them. Prophets like Amos condemned those who exploited the poor and vulnerable (Amos 5:11-12; see also Jeremiah 22:13 and Malachi 3:5). And no such acts today go unnoticed by him. The unpaid wages cry out to him; the cries of the harvesters reach his ears (James **5:4**). No one else may notice or care. But God sees, understands, and promises to act.

As James concludes his indictment, he saves his strongest charge for the end: "You have condemned and murdered the innocent one, who was not opposing you" (**v 6**). There is no reason to think this would not have been literally true. Wickedness and exploitation could directly have led to loss of life. Protesting workers could easily have been done away with, silenced for ever.

But it is also possible for the lifestyle of the wealthy to indirectly lead to the harm and even death of others. This is certainly the case in our own day. Those of us in the comparative wealth of the West need to reflect on our responsibility as consumers—to think about the kinds of companies we're supporting and how they treat their workers in far-flung and impoverished places. Wilful ignorance really is no defence. Our purchasing habits might well be furthering forms of injustice, and we have an opportunity to make a difference through the choices that we make. It is incumbent on us to care about such things and to do all we can to support upright companies and avoid those that deliberately hurt and exploit the economically vulnerable.

> We need to reflect on our responsibility as consumers— wilful ignorance is no defence.

So it is all too apparent why these rich people are to "weep and wail", and why such "misery ... is coming on" them (**v 1**). It is not wrong to be rich. The crime is not being wealthy, but hoarding, extravagance, and injustice. The problem is not having money, but loving money (1 Timothy 6:10).

Wealth is therefore dangerous. When we understand the judgment of God on such attitudes, we will think twice before wanting to be like the ungodly wealthy around us:

"Those who want to get rich fall into temptation and a trap and into many foolish and harmful desires that plunge people into ruin and destruction." (1 Timothy 6:9)

Covetousness will be less of a temptation to us when we realise what a trap worldly wealth can be. Perhaps James would encourage his readers, and us, to pray what the proverb encourages us to:

"Give me neither poverty nor riches, but give me only my daily bread. Otherwise, I may have too much and disown you and say, 'Who is the LORD?' Or I may become poor and steal, and so dishonour the name of my God." (Proverbs 30:8-9)

The world would mock such an ambition and request. God does not.

Questions for reflection

1. Do you see yourself in any of the description of the "worldly wealthy" in these verses?

2. Are there ways in which you aim to have things for yourself, rather than to use things for others? If so, how do you now have an opportunity to change your attitude and actions?

3. Why not pray Proverbs 30:8-9 daily and see how it changes your view of your wealth, and others' wealth?

9. PATIENCE IN SUFFERING

James now turns his attention from the rich to the poor, from the non-believer to the Christian, and from the oppressors to the oppressed. As usual, his counsel is direct, pithy and practical.

The Revolution will not be Christianised

James commands his readers—his "brothers and sisters"—to "be patient" (James **5:7**). For now, their lot seems to be one of injustice. They are among the workers and harvesters whose wages remain unpaid (v 4), and the innocent who are being run down and even destroyed by the opposition of the corrupt rich (v 6). This is, simply but sadly, the world in which they are living.

It is immediately apparent what their response is *not* to be. They are not to try to overturn the rich. However deserving they are of justice, they are not to resort to violence against their oppressors in order to achieve it. Their calling is to patience, not revolution. There is no call for the downtrodden workers of the world to rise up against the wealthy classes. Yet though this might horrify the Marxist, and even seem to underline their belief that religion like this is the opium of the masses, it is full of the practical wisdom we have come to expect from James. And we need to remember that James is writing for the sake of those who are suffering the most—as a Christian, to Christians—and the Christians were typically the ones on the receiving end of exploitation. James is not writing for the benefit of the establishment, trying to help them keep the people in check. His heart, his sympathies and his loyalties are to the ones facing appalling injustice. And his message to them is not one of revolution and overthrow, but of patience.

This call for patience flows directly from what James has just been teaching in the previous section: "Be patient, *then*..." James says (**v 7**). Patience is the application of what he has just said. Why? Because the cries of injustice do reach God's ears (v 4), and because there is a coming "day of slaughter" (v 5). The rationale is clear. In times of injustice it is easy to wonder if God has noticed, whether he cares, and why he is not working to intervene. James has just shown us that he has, he does, and he will. Christians do not need to take matters into their own hands. Justice will be done; even now it is being anticipated. These things are certain. James' readers need not fear for one moment that the unjust will get away with it.

> We need not fear for one moment that the unjust will get away with it.

This is why James ties his command to the coming return of Jesus: "Be patient, then ... until the Lord's coming" (**v 7**). For this is the event that will bring the promised justice. The coming of Jesus will not merely be an in-house event for his own people, by which they are able to join him for eternity. It will be a global and **cataclysmic** event. It will herald the judgment of all sin and the righting of all wrongs. It is the return of Jesus which will bring about the "day of slaughter" that James has just been promising.

In other words, this is not a call to patience without an end in sight. It is patience for a particular, defined period of time. James' readers will have the power to be patient precisely *because* the cause of their suffering will most certainly be thoroughly dealt with. They can afford to hang in there, knowing this is the case.

Imagine for a moment that a period of serious and sudden ill-health prompts a visit to the doctor and the diagnosis of a very unpleasant condition that will involve acute pain for some time. Also imagine that the doctor is emphatic that this condition is entirely curable. It will take several months, but a full recovery is certain. However painful the condition becomes, knowing it was only for a certain time will make it much easier to endure. You will have every reason to remain patient, and the motivation to do so. But just imagine trying to cope with those same circumstances without the prospect of full recovery. There would be none of the same impetus for patience. It would just be unremitting pain, with no end in sight. Patience would be far harder—and unwise action far likelier.

Knowing the end with confidence makes it possible to bear something otherwise virtually unendurable. James' readers can be patient because Jesus will return and their hardship will come to an end.

Waiting for the Rains

James provides an everyday example of the sort of patience he is calling for. *Think about the farmers*, he says (**v 7**). For people in James' day, farming was woven into the fabric of everyday life. If you were not an actual farmer yourself, you certainly knew many people who were. It was not a specialism at that time; it was how most people lived. James is therefore appealing to something that all of his readers would have been familiar with, as he points them to how a farmer "waits for the land to yield its valuable crop, patiently waiting for the autumn and spring rains" (**v 7**).

Rains in that part of the world came at two points of the year—the early rains in October/November after the crop was sown, and then another rainy period in March/April. Between these times, the farmer might need regularly to tend the ground and keep the weeds at bay, but he could do nothing at all to accelerate the process of bringing the crops to harvest. He had to wait. He knew the rain would come, and with it the harvest. It would happen, but it had not yet happened. He just needed to exercise patience—to wait with confidence.

This is not just a convenient illustration. The crop was "valuable" to the farmer because it would have been (by and large) the food his family depended on. The process of patiently waiting for the rain was part of survival. There was no other way to live.

Furthermore, James is making an important theological point in this. Knowing how well his predominantly Jewish readers knew the Old Testament, James could have been confident that they would have picked up the connection he was making to Deuteronomy 11:

> "So if you faithfully obey the commands I am giving you today—
> to love the LORD your God and to serve him with all your heart
> and with all your soul—then I will send rain on your land in its
> season, both autumn and spring rains, so that you may gather in
> your corn, new wine and olive oil." (v 13-14)

So this is not a "secular" analogy. James is not just appealing to "nature", saying that patience while waiting for God's justice is a bit like the farmer's patience with the weather. The regular rains are an expression of God's faithfulness. And just as he has repeatedly shown his faithfulness in sending rain at its time, so too he will show his faithfulness in bringing justice at the right time. *Just as you farmers are right to wait patiently in that instance,* James says, *so too you can do so in this.*

Stand Firm

But patience is not all James calls for (James **5:8**). By adding "stand firm" as he repeats his command, James is showing us what kind of patience is required of us. It is not passive. Waiting does not mean inactivity. While waiting for his harvest, the farmer would still do everything he could to ensure the health of his crop, working hard to clear weeds, add fertiliser, and so on. In the same way, Christians awaiting the justice to come are to do everything they can to strengthen and buttress their faith in God.

I'm not a particular fan of sumo wrestling but have caught enough clips on TV to get the general idea. Two (generally larger) gentlemen wrestle one another not in an attempt to knock the other out, but to move them out of the defined ring in which they both start the bout. Once one is pushed out, the other has won. The aim of the game, then, is the very thing James is commanding of us—to stand firm and hold our ground. Paul gives a similar exhortation in another context: "Stand firm. Let nothing move you" (1 Corinthians 15:58). And as with the world of sumo, so with the Christian life—such standing firm takes great determination. James is calling us to the opposite of laziness.

Once again, James grounds this instruction in the reality of the coming return of Jesus (James **5:8**). It is "near"; there is an imminence to Jesus' return that is to spur us on.

Some have suggested that these words mean that James, along with many other of the early Christians from his time, mistakenly expected the second coming of Jesus to be very soon—that he thought it would be within his lifetime, and based his teaching on this false expectation. Given how wrong he and others turned out to be on this, we mustn't take their teaching too seriously, the thinking goes. After all, it was based on a faulty understanding of when Jesus would come back. So his teaching cannot be authoritative, since he was mistaken on such an important point.

But this line of thought is to misunderstand James. He says that Christ's return is "near"; but that is not the same as saying that his return will "definitely be very soon". Nearness is not necessarily immediacy. Nearness means that little now stands in the way before it comes to fulfilment.

As I write, a small space probe called Rosetta has just completed a decade-long journey to get alongside and map a speeding comet. The journey has covered 6.4 billion kilometres, looping round the sun five times in the process. In relation to its journey overall, it would be fair to say that for the last several months Rosetta has been "near" its moving destination. The bulk of what needs to happen for it to complete its journey has happened; it is in its final stages. Yet all the while it remains (by our standards) a staggering distance from its target.

It is in this sense that the coming of Jesus is near. In relation to the whole process overall, the day of justice and judgment is not far off. The bulk of all that needed to happen beforehand has indeed happened. Jesus came in his **incarnation**, died, rose again and is now exalted at the right hand of the Father. Nothing else remains on God's calendar before Jesus' return. We are at the final stages, in the last days (v 3). The coming of Jesus was, for James, near. It remains near for us, two thousand years later.

And this nearness, notice, is the grounds for our standing firm. As was the case at the time of James, so too for us: it could happen at any moment. It is near. We are therefore to live in the light of that. James has one particular application in mind because our Judge "is standing at the door" (**v 9**). "Don't grumble against one another, brothers and sisters."

It is all too easy, when facing ongoing pressure, and even injustice in life, to turn against one another. We take out our frustration on our fellow believers, and vent our discontentment on them. It might be that we compare our own experience to that of other Christians around us, and sense that they know little of what we're going through, or that they're having an easier time of things than us. It can feel unfair. Or perhaps we're conscious of others facing trials that we know nothing of, and we feel they are not responding with the grace we think they should show (and, implicitly, that we assume we would show in their situation).

> It is the nearness of the Lord that is our impetus to live rightly.

Again, it is the nearness of the Lord that is our impetus to live rightly. The Judge is at the door—and it is hard to imagine him nearer than that. The handle is about to turn, and so we are to speak to one another in such a way that we would not be ashamed of the Lord Jesus himself being within earshot. This matters: James is clear that Jesus judges such grumbling (**v 9**). Such words are assessed by him. We are not to worry that our standing before God is threatened, but there is a clear implication here that Jesus is greatly displeased with us when we grumble.

So James has two instructions for his oppressed readers. They are to be patient, and they are to stand firm. In both cases, our impetus is the second coming. Its certainty means we can be patient, and its nearness prompts us to stand firm and hold our ground. He is coming, and he is near. We must wait, and wait well.

Questions for reflection

1. How does a firm grasp of God's coming justice change our view of our sufferings now?

2. Why is hard to think like this? Why is it liberating to do so?

3. How will you think and live differently today if you remember that "The Judge is at the door"?

PART TWO

The Prophets

Having provided clear instructions to his readers, James now goes on to provide worked examples for them and us to follow: the prophets in general (**v 10**) and Job in particular (**v 11**).

He begins with the prophets as an example of how to face suffering with patience. These examples serve a double purpose. First, they show that what James' readers are going through is not novel. This has been the lot of God's people through all generations. This present generation has no reason to think its own experience is an aberration.

We need reminding of this. It is possible for Western Christians especially to feel as though comfort and life going well are normal, and that hardship (expected or otherwise) is abnormal or even a sign that something must be wrong in our Christian lives. But the Bible nowhere leads us to have such an expectation; indeed, it is full of examples to the contrary. Suffering of one kind or another is normal for the people of God. It is not the sign that things have gone wrong, but that they've "gone normal".

Second, these examples serve to encourage us by showing how followers of God in the past have remained faithful in the very challenging situations in which they have found themselves. They have done the very things that James has just been calling his readers to do. They have remained faithful. And this shows that it is possible to be both patient and suffering. We can imagine being patient or suffering, but might struggle to see how the two could ever describe us in the same moment. By providing examples, James is saying it can be done. And by calling on such a category of examples, James shows that those able to do this are not the rare exception. This has been the **vocation** and experience of many, many people. If the experience of hardship itself is normative, so too is the godly response to it.

I once hiked up a volcano with some friends during a visit to Kenya. One or two others we had spoken to had recommended the experience. It wasn't typically part of the tourist trail, they said, but was well worth trying to do. We all liked the idea that we would be doing something most other visitors would not have thought of doing. It seemed somehow a little more exclusive.

> Suffering is not the sign that things have gone wrong, but that they've gone normal.

This feeling was certainly reinforced by the climb itself. The route up was challenging in the dust and heat of the Rift Valley. As we crested the summit and enjoyed the view, we felt a little like explorers, going where few others had been before. Such feelings came to an abrupt halt. Looking back along the trial we had taken, we could see a line of people coming up, and at a considerably quicker pace than we had managed. As they approached the top, we realised it was a party of young schoolchildren, on a school trip to visit the volcano. We suddenly felt a lot less heroic. It turned out even kids had done what we'd just done.

It is part of our arrogant, sinful nature to assume that we are the first generation ever truly to experience what we're going through. James wants his readers to be very clear that what they are facing, while by no means easy, is certainly not new. Those who suffer as Christians are not blazing a new trail, but travelling a well worn path. And if their experience is not novel, then James' counsel to them is not unrealistic. The prophets have gone through all this before—and they've been faithful. Not only have they responded to their suffering with patience, but James reminds us that they "spoke in the name of the Lord" (**v 10**). They did their job, and ministered to God's people, *while* they were suffering, rather than waiting till the suffering stopped. To those prone to using their tongues to grumble against each other, this is a wonderful encouragement to put them to far better use. What James is calling us to do is therefore neither novel nor impossible; and it does not render us incapable of either serving or witnessing.

It is easy to see why, of all God's people in the Old Testament, James chose the prophets as an example for his readers. They were not the only ones required to show patience in the face of suffering, but it did seem to typify their experience. Suffering went with the turf. Speaking in the name of the Lord meant saying things that people did not want to hear; it required them to expose the sins and injustices of the people of their day. For many prophets, this meant directly challenging the king himself. It is no surprise that virtually every prophet we know anything about exercised his ministry at considerable personal cost. Between them they experienced it all (perhaps an echo of the "trials of many kinds" that James' own readers are facing, 1:2).

Suffering does not render us incapable of either serving or witnessing.

James does not specify which particular prophets he has in mind, but it's hard to imagine he isn't thinking of Jeremiah, among others. His was an especially unhappy ministry. He was tasked to explain the impending judgment that God was about to bring on his people—conquest by and captivity in the Babylonian Empire. For this message, Jeremiah suffered enormously. His own family betrayed him (Jeremiah 12:6), he was beaten and put into stocks by a temple official (20:2), imprisoned by the king (37:18), threatened with death (38:4), and thrown into a cistern (38:6). Yet throughout all of this, Jeremiah remained faithful to his calling, speaking the word of God, and by doing so demonstrated the very patience that James has been commending. Jeremiah's experience, though acute, was not atypical. Such was the calling of a prophet of God. And such is the example for the people of God.

Were that not enough for his readers to mull over, James adds a further challenge: that "we count as blessed those who have persevered" (James **5:11**). The fact is that the Christians to whom James was writing had long celebrated such examples from the Old Testament. They themselves had reflected on the blessing found by those who had faithfully come through suffering. Jesus himself said:

"Blessed are you when people insult you, persecute you and falsely say all kinds of evil against you because of me" (Matthew 5:11). James too has already told his readers: "Blessed is the one who perseveres under trial" (James 1:12). Trials, James has shown us, are the very means that God can use to grow our faith and deepen our dependence on him. They are a necessary (if uncomfortable) part of Christian maturity. When they come, we are not to resent them, but to see how God might use them to be a means of blessing. A life free of all such trials will never produce the depth and maturity that God longs to see in his people—and which we, in our better moments, know we so very much need.

Job

James then moves on to his second example, Job. His patience has become proverbial, and was evidently well known by James' readers (**5:11**). Job is an example of someone who lost everything—his possessions, his family, and his health. Even his friends, in their attempts to provide comfort, ended up adding to his woes. Yet through it all, Job persevered. He remained faithful to God. Throughout the book of Job, amid all his personal turmoil and pronounced spiritual ups and downs (mainly downs), we see repeated evidence of his faith in God:

> "[Job] said: 'Naked I came from my mother's womb, and naked I shall depart. The LORD gave and the LORD has taken away; may the name of the LORD be praised.'" (Job 1:21)

> "His wife said to him, 'Are you still maintaining your integrity? Curse God and die!'

> "He replied, 'You are talking like a foolish woman. Shall we accept good from God, and not trouble?'" (2:9-10)

> "Even now my witness is in heaven; my advocate is on high ... on behalf of a man he pleads with God as one pleads for a friend." (16:19, 21)

"I know that my redeemer lives, and that in the end he will stand
on the earth. And after my skin has been destroyed, yet in my
flesh I will see God; I myself will see him with my own eyes—
I, and not another." (19:25-27)

Through all his sufferings, though he complained bitterly about his
plight, Job never cursed God. His faith, though at times weak, was
nevertheless true. God even praised Job for how he spoke (42:7). He
persevered.

James now turns from Job's faith to Job's eventual outcome—
"what the Lord finally brought about" (James **5:11**). James' readers
knew well Job's perseverance; they also knew of the prosperity he
came to enjoy at the end. His sufferings, intense as they were, were
not the end of the story. His situation was transformed, as a tangible
and material expression of how "the Lord is full of compassion and
mercy" (**v 11**).

It is not hard to see the relevance of this for James' readers. The
point is not that God will invariably bless his suffering people with
material prosperity in this life. We see too many examples in the history of God's people where this is demonstrably not the case (a point
expanded by the writer to the Hebrews, eg: 11:35b-38). The point is
that Job persevered, and God in his compassion and mercy blessed
him. That same compassion and mercy will be evident as God blesses
those in our own day who press on with faith as Job did.

What does your "Yes" Mean?

These two examples—the prophets and Job—press home the possibility and goodness of exercising the kind of patience that James
has been commending. Many have gone before us and have suffered
greatly as God's people. And many too have shown great spiritual in-
tegrity as they have done so, remaining faithful to God and continuing
with their ministries even through desperate trials. If they were able
to persevere, then we—for whom the return of Jesus is both more
certain and closer—can and should follow in their footsteps.

But James is not done yet. Once again he turns our attention to the significance of how we speak in such times. Twice we are reminded in this short section of how, as we seek to wait patiently in the trials of this life, our tongues have the capacity to spoil everything. And once again, he attaches a solemn warning: "Above all, my brothers and sisters, do not swear—not by heaven or by earth or by anything else. All you need to say is a simple 'Yes' or 'No'. Otherwise you will be condemned" (James **5:12**).

Earlier we were warned against grumbling (**v 9**). Now we are told not to swear oaths. James is not abruptly changing subjects here. His prohibition against swearing is a further application of the patience that he has been calling for through this section. As we wait with patience, we are to speak with patience. Rash speech can quickly threaten godly endurance.

James is returning to his theme of consistency in the Christian life. The swearing of oaths is another expression of the double-mindedness that has been characterising many of his readers and undermining the credibility of their Christian confession. The particular oaths that James has in mind seem to involve invoking God's name to underline the reliability of a promise. We can imagine how easily this might happen among believers suffering the sorts of economic hardships that James has been describing. Unrealistic vows made in the heat of the moment will easily be broken.

Oaths are not universally condemned in Scripture. God himself on occasion swears by oath (eg: Acts 2:30). Paul at times calls God to be his witness that what he is writing is true (eg: 2 Corinthians 1:23). The point is not that all oaths are always wrong, but that in everyday contexts oaths should be unnecessary. We shouldn't need to emphasise the truthfulness of a particular part of our speech, because all our speech should be true and trustworthy. James is not ruling out Christians speaking under oath in a courtroom, but ruling out ever needing to outside of one. Everything we say should be true. Our word should be enough.

10. PRAYERS THAT CHANGE THINGS

This last section of James is well acknowledged as being one of the hardest to understand in the whole letter (and perhaps even the whole New Testament!). A couple of years ago when I was preaching through the letter, one church member came up to me with some concern and asked if we were going to be looking at "the dodgy bit at the end", by which they meant these final verses of James 5. Another member was equally concerned that we might miss it out.

Whatever challenges particular passages of Scripture might present, we must never skip over them. Given what we know about the divine inspiration of Scripture, it won't do to say it's the fault of the passage; the text is exactly as God meant it to be. If we find it hard to understand, it is surely because the problem is with us and not the passage. This should mean we come to it with both humility (since our confusion shows we have a lot to learn) and determination (since we know God has inspired this text for our benefit and learning).

Ruling Options Out

With any "difficult" text, it helps to rule out what it can't mean. These verses include discussion of prayer (**v 13-18**) and, within those, healing (**v 14-16**). The detail is clear enough to show us what it isn't about.

First, these verses clearly are not describing the Roman Catholic practice of extreme unction, or last rites. This is a practice whereby someone thought to be on their deathbed is anointed with oil by a priest, makes their confession, and is therefore (spiritually) saved

eliminate the impossible and what remains, however unlikely, must be the truth!

Prayer is Always the Answer

James begins this section with the importance of prayer (once again). He describes a range of circumstances that a believer might find themselves in—"in trouble … happy … ill" (**v 13-14**). In each case, the response is to pray. Life is always going to be a mixture of ups and downs, but the constant among Christians is to be how we respond— we are to bring it all before the Lord, whether in praise or prayer. There is no situation in life where prayer to God is not relevant or right. Our whole lives are to be lived in relation to God. There's never a time when it's not good to pray. So, why not now? Take a moment to reflect on your own situation and bring it to God in prayer.

And that includes times of sickness, to which James turns to focus upon in more detail. As ever, it is important to understand the context in which this discussion of sickness and healing takes place. While the letter of James might not be as tightly structured as, say, Paul's letter to the Romans, there is nevertheless a flow to it. It is not haphazard. James is not flinging unrelated snippets of wisdom at the reader. It is not that he woke up on this particular morning thinking: *I'm going to write some stuff today about healing.* No—these verses relate to what James has been saying all along, to the concerns he has been outlining in the course of the letter, and to the conclusion of it all to which he will shortly come.

The great pressing issues behind this letter are spiritual drifting— what James has called double-mindedness and spiritual adultery—and of the need to come back to God in wholehearted faith. It is in this context that James discusses sickness. He is not necessarily saying that every time someone from church sneezes, the elders need to come round with grapes and prayer. More likely, James is addressing sickness that comes in a particular context which warrants the ministry of the church leadership. In the verses that follow, James seems to identify sickness with sin, and healing with repentance:

- The prayer offered ... will make the sick person well [literally, *sosei*—'saved']" (**5:15**).

- "Confess your sins ... so that you may be healed" (**v 16**).

Notice that the results appear the "wrong way round" here—the sick person is saved, and the sinner is healed. We would ordinarily expect this to say that the sick person will be healed and the sinner saved. But James is drawing a connection between the person's sickness and their sin.

The New Testament urges great caution in making this sort of connection. In general, sickness is part and parcel of life in a broken and fallen world. It is part of the fallout of our collective rebellion against God, and in that sense is indiscriminate—we experience sickness because we live in a sinful world, and not necessarily because we have been particularly sinful. Jesus warned his disciples about assuming someone's affliction was the result of particular sin (John 9:1-3).

But there are some occasions in the New Testament where sickness is the result of sin. Jesus warned the healed invalid: "See, you are well again. Stop sinning or something worse may happen to you" (John 5:14). A failure to repent raises the possibility of further and more extreme affliction. Similarly, Paul writes to the wayward believers in Corinth:

"Everyone ought to examine themselves before they eat of the bread and drink from the cup. For those who eat and drink without discerning the body of Christ eat and drink judgment on themselves. *That is why many among you are weak and ill, and a number of you have fallen asleep*." (1 Corinthians 11:28-30, emphasis added)

There can be a connection between sickness and sin, when the former is discipline from God for the latter. In the example James is about to give from the time of Elijah, God's discipline on his people was to

Questions for reflection

1. To what extent is prayer your first response to both the ups and the downs of life? Why is this, do you think?

2. Do you think you are tempted to be too quick, or too slow, to connect adverse circumstances to unrepentant sin? What are the strengths and dangers of such an approach?

3. How would you answer the questions in the paragraph above? How would you like to be able to answer them?

PART TWO

Powerful and Effective

James has reminded us of the importance of prayer in our Christian lives in general (**v 13**), and in the context of repentance in particular (**v 14-16**). We all have a role to play in this, whether in confessing to others or in praying for others, and over time most likely in both. Either way, all of us are to be people who pray. We need to realise and remember that praying is not merely a kind gesture for someone else. It makes all the difference, for "the prayer of a righteous person is powerful and effective" (**v 16**).

Prayer can actually do things. Our prayers change things. If we are righteous—walking in the grace of God—we have the opportunity to make a huge difference in the lives of others, and especially among the people of God.

As is his habit, James offers us an example: the seminal Old Testament prophet Elijah, one of the most important figures in Israel's history, and yet who was, as James points out, "a human being, even as we are" (**v 17a**).

Reading through the life and ministry of Elijah (in 1 Kings 17 – 2 Kings 2), we might be tempted to question just how true this is! He is a famous prophet for a reason. God performed some spectacular miracles through him. Perhaps the most well known is when Elijah confronted the prophets of the false god Baal, challenging them to a contest to see whether their god or his would bring fire upon the sacrifice each of them had prepared (you can read the account of this in 1 Kings 18). Knowing God would answer his prayer, Elijah even soaked his altar with water to underline the supernatural element of what was about to happen. This is hardly a typical day in the office for the Christian!

But in James 5, it is not the *miracles* of Elijah which James wants us to focus on, but rather, the *prayer* of Elijah. James is citing Elijah precisely because this great Old Testament prophet is a wonderful

have had, to be left clutching the equivalent of a pair of socks that we never even realised we would get. Not every Christian can be a great theologian, preacher, missionary or evangelist. But every Christian can be a great and effective pray-er.

Prayers God Loves to Hear

There is another, deeper point that James is making. The things Elijah prayed for were not arbitrary. He didn't ask for drought because he was fed up with all the drizzle and needed some bright sunshine. Nor did he pray for rain because he realized his flowers were beginning to fade. Elijah's prayers came in a context especially significant for the point James is making. First, as we've seen, it was a time of enormous spiritual adultery under the reign of Ahab. Second, drought and rain are significant in the Old Testament. God had said, early on in the life of Israel, that if they turned away from him, he would send certain punishments, one of which was drought: "The LORD will strike you with ... scorching heat and drought ... The sky over your head will be bronze, the ground beneath you iron" (Deuteronomy 28:22-23).

It is because of this that Elijah had the confidence to declare to Ahab: "As the LORD, the God of Israel, lives, whom I serve, there will be neither dew nor rain in the next few years except at my word" (1 Kings 17:1). The drought God's people experienced was not just bad luck, but judgment on sin. It was a shot across the bows—an expression of judgment in their present to wake them up to the reality of what they were doing so that they might turn and be spared greater judgment in the future.

And the particular sin behind their rebellion was very clear. Elijah put it bluntly: "How long will you waver between two opinions? If the LORD is God, follow him; but if Baal is God, follow him" (1 Kings 18:21).

This should ring a bell—because it is exactly the same issue James had identified in his readers. The people of Israel were wavering between two opinions—they were double-minded, trying to have a foot in each camp, hoping to get what God could give them and to take what Baal could give them. It is the same problem that has been behind so much of what James has written in his letter. And it was because of this that Elijah prayed for God to discipline them—for rain to be withheld—and then, after there was repentance and a wholehearted worship of the LORD, he prayed for that discipline to be lifted and for the people to be restored—for rain to return.

So yes, Elijah reminds us of the power of prayer; but he reminds us of the power of prayer in a particular context—bringing doubleminded sinners back to God. In other words, our prayers are powerful when they are prayed in line with God's purposes and promises. That is why it is the prayers of a "righteous" person that are "powerful and effective" (James **5:16**)—because the more we are shaped by God's grace to us in Christ, the more we will become like Christ, longing for the honour of God's name and the increase of his kingdom, praying the first lines of the Lord's Prayer because we desire to rather than because we are told to. It is a wonderful privilege to pray according to God's purposes as they become our own desires; and then watch our prayers change things as God responds to our prayers.

And God is in the business of rescuing lost sheep (Luke 15:3-7). So was Elijah, and so should we be. It is to this vital ministry that James turns for the final words of this letter, for the ministry Elijah had to the people of God is one we are all to have to one another.

> "My brothers and sisters, if one of you should wander from the truth and someone should bring that person back, remember this: whoever turns a sinner from the error of their way will save them from death and cover over a multitude of sins."

> (James **5:19-20**)

James shows us the seriousness of wandering from the truth, and this is no small matter. James says it risks death (**v 20**). To wander from the truth is to wander from life.

But the trouble is that wandering doesn't feel risky at the time; it feels like being adventurous, exploring a little, getting off the beaten track. We do not know we have made a mistake until it is too late, and we look back and see that adventure was in fact folly.

This is true for us spiritually, too. Being double-minded does not feel dangerous. If feels like getting the best of both worlds, like being relevant, like enjoying all that life has to offer. And it seems even less dangerous when others around us are doing a similar thing. We can't *all* be wrong, right? Yet it is all too easy for an unspoken rule to emerge in our churches indicating that a level of worldliness in particular contexts is tolerable and even encouraged. What that level is will vary from church to church and culture to culture. It might concern greed, or materialism, or gossip, or lust, or worry, or any number of other things which God tells us not to do, but which the world around us encourages and celebrates.

But however comfortable it might feel, to wander from the truth is to wander towards death. It is spiritual suicide. Either wandering will keep you from the truth, or the truth will keep you from wandering.

Search-and-Rescue and You

When there is this kind of wandering in our churches—and there will be—we are to go on spiritual search-and-rescue missions. "If ... someone should bring that person back..." (**v 19**)—my brother or sister's wandering is not just their problem; it is mine. We are to urge the wanderer to come back to wholehearted faith, loving God with their whole life. It might be someone close to us, or a member of a Bible-study group. It might be someone from church, and we're conscious we've not seen them for a while. It might be an ungodly relationship they're in, or the pursuit of ungodly priorities. Whatever it is, trying to "bring that person back" from such a departure from the truth is not easy. In fact it can feel incredibly awkward. Living in the UK, it is thought to be very un-British to confront someone over something personal, however gently and appropriately it is done. It is not really part of our culture—or, to be honest, our church culture— to involve ourselves in the personal affairs of others. It is thought to be meddling and a sign of self-righteousness. We've always been taught to mind our own business. And in any case, we don't like conflict. We don't like to risk a relationship or cause a scene. We'd rather keep out of things.

But whatever our cultural reservations, James is unequivocal. I'm not called to be English; I'm called to be Christian. And part of that calling is to seek to restore the spiritual wanderer. Notice that it is not just the responsibility of the church leader. James is addressing his "brothers and sisters" (**v 19**). It is "one of you" that might wander; it is "someone" that is needed to bring them back. We must not tell ourselves that it is just the role of the pastor or leader. If the wanderer is a Christian brother or sister, and you know it is happening, then it is *your* responsibility to call them back.

It needs to be done carefully, of course. Paul has the following help for us on this: "Brothers and sisters [notice who he, too, is addressing], if someone is caught in a sin, you who live by the Spirit should restore that person gently. But watch yourselves, or you also may be tempted" (Galatians 6:1).

We need to be humble. It is only by God's grace that we are not in that situation ourselves, and we may well have been so on other occasions. There is a need for gentleness and self-examination. It needs to be done carefully, prayerfully and lovingly; but it does need to be done. And the wonder of the gospel is that it *can* be done. It may risk the friendship, even if done with love. It may cause offence, even if done with care. But it is worth doing. You may end up saving a life; for the death of Jesus—the Lord Jesus of the glory (James 2:1)—

> There is always a way back, because at the cross there is always hope.

can and does "cover over a multitude of sins" (**5:20**). You know that, because you know it covers yours. If you call someone back from wandering away from the cross and towards hell, you are literally saving their eternal life. There is always a way back, because at the cross there is always hope for the double-minded. There is always hope for us all. Whatever else you do, "remember this," says James (**v 20**).

Questions for reflection

1. How does thinking about Elijah's prayers excite you about yours?

2. Is there a "wanderer" you need to seek to "bring ... back" today? Or do you need someone to challenge you in some way?

3. James' letter is a deeply practical part of Scripture. How has the Spirit been prompting you to love Jesus more, and work harder and more wholeheartedly in living for him?

GLOSSARY

Addendum: item of additional material.

Analogy: a comparison between two things, usually using one of them to explain or clarify the other.

Apostle: a man appointed directly by the risen Christ to teach about him with authority.

Archetypal: completely typical; best example.

Atypical: not at all normal (the opposite of archetypal).

Beatitude: an explanation of how to live in a way that is blessed.

Blessed: enjoy satisfaction and fulfilment; to live the best way possible, and the way that God designed us to live.

Brevity: briefness, conciseness.

Cataclysmic: enormous, earth-shattering.

Conservative: a label given to churches that view the Bible as written by God and without mistakes.

Corporate: shared; something that is done by a group, not an individual.

Counselled: advised; taught.

Creed: a formal statement of Christian belief (eg: the Apostles' Creed, the Nicene Creed).

Cross-reference: two or more places in the Bible that link to one another (eg: James 2:8 is a cross-reference to both Leviticus 19:18 and Mark 12:29-31).

Discern: perceive, see the truth, understand.

Divine inspiration: the belief that all of the Bible was inspired by God, so that the humans writing the words wrote exactly what he intended them to (see 2 Timothy 3:15-17; 2 Peter 1 v 20-21).

Elders: men who are responsible for the teaching and ministry of a church.

Ethics: a set of moral principles. **Biblical ethics** are moral principles based entirely on the teaching of the Bible.

Evangelist: someone who equips other Christians to tell non-Christians the gospel of Jesus Christ, and who is gifted at doing this themselves.

Executive summary: a short summary of a longer document.

Exhortation: strong encouragement or urging to change or continue something.

Faith: a real, whole-hearted trust in Jesus as King and Saviour.

"Fallen asleep": a phrase Paul sometimes uses to speak of Christian's dying.

Genre: category or type.

Gospel: an announcement, often translated "good news". When the Roman Emperor sent a proclamation around the empire declaring a victory or achievement, this was called a "gospel". The gospel is good news to be believed, not advice to be followed.

Growbags: bags of fertilised soil, used to help plants grow rapidly.

Humiliation: humble-ness; a process of making someone think less highly of themselves.

Hypothetical: an imaginary situation that is realistic, but not real.

Incarnation: the coming of the divine Son of God as a human, in the person of Jesus of Nazareth.

Justified: the status of being not guilty, not condemned, completely innocent.

Mandated: commanded, ordered.

Marxist: someone who follows the theories of Karl Marx and Friedrich Engels, part of which is the pursuing of the revolutionary overthrow of capitalist systems by the workers, in order to set up a classless society.

Nominalism: a belief or view held in name only. A nominal Manchester

United fan would be one whose actions and emotions are rarely, if ever, shaped by the team's results, and who never accepts a cost or sacrificial commitment to support the team.

Oracles: divine messages, communicated through a human.

Orthodox: standard, accepted Christian teaching.

Parable: a memorable story that illustrates a truth about Jesus and/or his kingdom.

Patriarch: the "first fathers" of Israel, to whom God gave his promises—Abraham, Isaac and Jacob.

Pentecost: a Jewish feast celebrating God giving his people his law on Mount Sinai (Exodus 19 – 31). On the day of this feast, fifty days after Jesus' resurrection, the Holy Spirit came to the first Christians (Acts 2), and so "Pentecost" is how Christians tend to refer to this event.

Perseveres: continues to think or do something, despite facing difficulties.

Philanthropist: someone who tries to promote the welfare of others, particularly by donating money.

Prodigal son: the younger son in Jesus' parable in Luke 15:11-32, who leaves his father's house, spends his inheritance, returns in shame, and finds his father ready to welcome and embrace him.

Promised land: the land on the eastern coast of the Mediterranean Sea that God promised Abraham he would give his descendants (Genesis 12:6-8; 13:14-18)

QED: it is proven (stands for the Latin phrase "quod erat demonstrandum").

Reformer: one of the first two generations of people in the sixteenth and early-seventeenth centuries who preached the gospel of justification by faith, and opposed the Pope and the Roman church.

Rhetorical device: a technique used by a speaker or writer to try to persuade the listener or reader to see an issue in a different way.

Secular: something (or someone) that does not refer to God or religion.

Sound doctrine: correct statement(s) concerning what is true about God.

Spurious: something that isn't what it appears to be, but rather is false, fake; and is therefore useless or invalid.

Theology: the study of what is true about God.

Trials: James means testing periods of life; eg: a time of ill-health, or persecution, or loneliness, or unemployment

Vocation: calling.

BIBLIOGRAPHY

- Craig L. Blomberg and Mariam J. Kamell, *James* in the Zondervan Exegetical Commentary on the New Testament Series (Zondervan, 2008)

- John Calvin, *Commentaries on the Catholic Epistles (James)*, translated John Owen (reprint: Baker Books, 1999)

- John Dickson, *James: The Wisdom of the Brother of Jesus* (Aquila Press, 2006)

- Douglas Moo, *The Letter of James* in the Pillar New Testament Commentary (Eerdmans/Apollos, 2000)

- Alec Motyer, *James: The Tests of Faith* in The Bible Speaks Today series (IVP, 1985)

- J.C. Ryle, *Thoughts for Young Men* (Calvary Press, 1993)

- George M. Stulac, *James* in the New Testament Commentary series (IVP, 1993)

- Rico Tice, *Honest Evangelism* (The Good Book Company, 2015)

James for...
Bible-study Groups

Sam Allberry's *Good Book Guide* to James is the companion to this resource, helping groups of Christians to explore, discuss and apply the book together. Six studies, each including investigation, apply, getting personal, pray and explore more sections, take you through the whole book of James. Includes a concise Leader's Guide at the back.

Find out more at:
www.thegoodbook.com/goodbookguides

Daily Devotionals

Explore daily devotional helps you open up the Scriptures and will encourage and equip you in your walk with God. Available as a quarterly booklet, *Explore* is also available as an app, where you can download Sam's notes on James, alongside contributions from trusted Bible teachers including Timothy Keller, Mark Dever, Tim Chester, Albert Mohler, Jr., and Juan Sanchez.

Find out more at:
www.thegoodbook.com/explore

More For You

Galatians For You

"The book of Galatians is dynamite. It is an explosion of joy and freedom which leaves us enjoying a life of blessing. I pray that it explodes in your heart as you read this book."

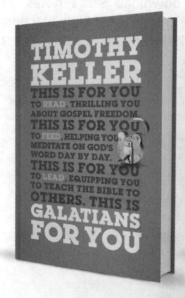

Daniel For You

"The book of Daniel offers you the knowledge that God is still at work, the confidence that it is possible to remain faithful to Jesus Christ, and the strength to live for him in our day."

The Whole Series

- **Exodus For You**
  Tim Chester
- **Judges For You**
  Timothy Keller
- **1 Samuel For You**
  Tim Chester
- **2 Samuel For You**
  Tim Chester
- **Psalms For You**
  Christopher Ash
- **Proverbs For You**
  Kathleen Nielson
- **Daniel For You**
  David Helm
- **Micah For You**
  Stephen Um
- **Luke 1-12 For You**
  Mike McKinley
- **Luke 12-24 For You**
  Mike McKinley
- **John 1-12 For You**
  Josh Moody
- **John 13-21 For You**
  Josh Moody
- **Acts 1-12 For You**
  Albert Mohler

- **Acts 13-28 For You**
  Albert Mohler
- **Romans 1-7 For You**
  Timothy Keller
- **Romans 8-16 For You**
  Timothy Keller
- **2 Corinthians For You**
  Gary Millar
- **Galatians For You**
  Timothy Keller
- **Ephesians For You**
  Richard Coekin
- **Philippians For You**
  Steven Lawson
- **Colossians & Philemon For You**
  Mark Meynell
- **1 & 2 Timothy For You**
  Phillip Jensen
- **Titus For You**
  Tim Chester
- **James For You**
  Sam Allberry
- **1 Peter For You**
  Juan Sanchez
- **Revelation For You**
  Tim Chester

Find out more about these resources at:
www.thegoodbook.com/for-you

Good Book Guides
for groups and individuals

Judges: The flawed and the flawless

Timothy Keller
Senior Pastor, Redeemer Presbyterian Church, Manhattan

Welcome to a time when God's people were deeply flawed, often failing, and struggling to live in a world which worshipped other gods. Our world is not so different—we need Judges to equip us to live for God in our day, and remind us that he is a God of patience and mercy.
Also by Tim Keller: Romans 1–7; Romans 8–16; Galatians

Daniel: Staying strong in a hostile world

David Helm
Lead Pastor, Holy Trinity Church, Chicago

The first half of Daniel is well known and much loved. The second is little read and less understood! David Helm leads groups through the whole book, showing how the truths about God in the second half enabled Daniel and his friends—and will inspire us—to live faithful, courageous lives.

Esther: Royal rescue

Jane McNabb
Chair of the London Women's Convention

The experience of God's people in Esther's day helps us in those moments when we question God's sovereignty, his love, or his faithfulness. Their story reveals that despite appearances, God is in control, and he answers his people's prayers—often in most unexpected ways.

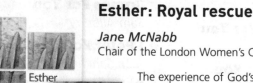

1 Corinthians 1–9: Challenging church

Mark Dever
Senior Pastor of Capitol Hill Baptist Church in
Washington DC and President of 9Marks Ministries

The church in Corinth was full of life, and just as
full of problems. As you read how Paul challenges
these Christians, you'll see how you can
contribute to your own church becoming truly
shaped by the gospel.
Also by Mark Dever: 1 Corinthians 10–16

James: Genuine faith

Sam Allberry
Associate Minister, St Mary's Maidenhead, UK

Many Christians long for a deeper, more wholehearted Christian life. But what does that look like?
This deeply practical letter was written to show us,
and will reveal how to experience joy in hardships,
patience in suffering and whole-heartedness in how
you speak, act and pray.
Also by Sam Allberry: Man of God; Biblical Manhood

1 Peter: Living well on the way home

Juan Sanchez
Preaching Pastor, High Pointe Baptist Church, Austin, Texas

The Christian life, lived well, is not easy—because
we don't belong in this world. Learn from Peter
how to journey on rather than retreat, and to do
so with joy and hope, rather than gritted teeth.

thegoodbook
COMPANY

BIBLICAL | RELEVANT | ACCESSIBLE

At The Good Book Company, we are dedicated to helping Christians and local churches grow. We believe that God's growth process always starts with hearing clearly what he has said to us through his timeless word—the Bible.

Ever since we opened our doors in 1991, we have been striving to produce Bible-based resources that bring glory to God. We have grown to become an international provider of user-friendly resources to the Christian community, with believers of all backgrounds and denominations using our books, Bible studies, devotionals, evangelistic resources, and DVD-based courses.

We want to equip ordinary Christians to live for Christ day by day, and churches to grow in their knowledge of God, their love for one another, and the effectiveness of their outreach.

Call us for a discussion of your needs or visit one of our local websites for more information on the resources and services we provide.

Your friends at The Good Book Company

thegoodbook.com | thegoodbook.co.uk
thegoodbook.com.au | thegoodbook.co.nz
thegoodbook.co.in